# CONVERSATIONS WITH SPIRIT

## THE TRUTH ABOUT DEATH AND REINCARNATION

ROBERT H. SKYE AND BRONWEN SKYE

Copyright © 2019
Robert H. Skye
& Bronwen Skye
Conversations
With
Spirit
The Truth About Death and Reincarnation
All rights reserved.

No part of this publication may be reproduced, distributed, or transmitted in any form or by any means, including photocopying, recording, or other electronic or mechanical methods, without the prior written permission of the publisher, except in the case of brief quotations embodied in critical reviews and certain other non-commercial uses permitted by copyright law.

Vireo Publishing

Printed in the United States of America
First Printing 2019
First Edition 2019

10 9 8 7 6 5 4 3 2 1

Paperback ISBN: 978-1-7984149-3-4
Hardcover ISBN: 979-8-9878377-0-2

# DEDICATION

- We would like to dedicate this book to Paris Davis for being the catalyst for a wonderful spiritual journey.

- We would also like to dedicate this to all the unseen souls who have helped make this book a reality.

*It has been my pleasure and one of the most exciting and enlightening experiences to meet the entity channeled by my wife, Bronwen.*

*--Robert H. Skye*

*We hope you enjoy this material. If you do and are searching for more, go to* **skyedialogues.com** *for our latest publications including our next book,*

*Karmic Law of Attraction:*
*A Channeled Explanation of Auras and Positive Living*

# TABLE OF CONTENTS

INTRODUCTION BY ........................................................................... *i*
ROBERT H. SKYE
INTRODUCTION BY .......................................................................... *v*
BRONWEN SKYE
CHAPTER 1 .......................................................................................... 1
  WHO AM I? I AM YOU
CHAPTER 2 ........................................................................................ 11
  THE NATURE OF THE SOUL
CHAPTER 3 ........................................................................................ 27
  DREAMS
CHAPTER 4 ........................................................................................ 45
  YOU ARE NOT REINCARNATED
CHAPTER 5 ........................................................................................ 59
  THE LIFE EXPERIENCE
CHAPTER 6 ........................................................................................ 77
  PROBABLE SELVES AND THE NATURE OF PROBABILITIES
CHAPTER 7 ........................................................................................ 99
  THE DEATH EXPERIENCE
CHAPTER 8 ...................................................................................... 119
  SYSTEMS AFTER DEATH
CHAPTER 9 ...................................................................................... 145
  ATTACHMENTS IN THE PHYSICAL AND BEYOND
CHAPTER 10 .................................................................................... 159
  YOUR CHEERLEADING SECTION
CHAPTER 11 .................................................................................... 191
  HUMAN EVOLUTION
CHAPTER 12 .................................................................................... 209
  OUR RELATIONSHIPS WITH ANIMALS

# INTRODUCTION BY ROBERT H. SKYE

Have you ever wondered what happens to our souls when we die? Where do souls come from? How is a soul different from consciousness? I have had the privilege of discussing these questions with a non-physical spiritual entity. I have found some logical answers that really make sense. It turns out there is more fun to be had after we die.

This book is the culmination of the many conversations I have had with the spiritual entities that collectively call themselves Brahma. No, this is not the Hindu god Brahma, nor is it Brahma chickens or Brahma bulls. It is only the name that one group of larger souls has chosen based on phonetic preference.

These conversations with Brahma were channeled through my wonderfully unique wife, Bronwen. She first became interested in channeling after her brother died, which triggered an intense search for spiritual meaning. Perhaps this attracted Brahma to her or maybe it somehow brought to the surface an aspect of her own spiritual greater entity. I don't fully understand how it works but I do know that I got some really good answers to my questions.

The identity of Brahma is impossible to prove, but I can testify that the information we have uncovered is meaningful and insightful. For anyone in search of answers about the nature of our souls and our incarnations in this reality, this book is for you.

By its very nature, the content of spiritual writing is largely unprovable. But I believe that most of us have an innate ability to sense truth after sufficient understanding of the concepts of any subject matter. In this manner, I hope you will see the validity of the material that will help in understanding our physical world as well as the spiritual one.

I have always questioned things, and I've been accused of playing devil's advocate many times. In college I sharpened my skepticism and agnosticism while I worked on my degree in philosophy. When I was younger, I believed only what I saw and what I could deduce logically. Mathematics and science were my religion.

## Introduction

But as I have grown older, I have become open to much more spiritual truths. I have come to the conclusion that there is too much happening in the world that cannot be explained by science. Metaphysical naturalism or the idea that only nature is real is a much too narrow viewpoint. One day the true nature of the universe may be understood scientifically in terms of energy as well as physical matter. But today's narrow view of science and physics does not account for the countless instances of people exhibiting psychic ability and knowing or perceiving things they should not—at least according to conventional standards—be able to know or sense.

We may someday find provable explanations for supernatural phenomena. But this proof will have to allow for the existence of a spiritual world in our universe. Psychics are not getting information from their sense of smell or through microscopic messages. Nature does not explain everything.

Over the course of several years, I recorded the conversations I had with Brahma as channeled by Bronwen Skye. I transcribed each session and with the help of both Brahma and Bronwen, I have compiled the topics into chapters. I have left it mostly in the question-and-answer format in hopes that the reader will be able to follow the information as it was presented to me. Although I have cut out much of the personal advice that I have received, I did leave in some personal content in places where it helps to illustrate the concepts. For example, we discuss the names of some of my spirit guides as well as the name of my larger entity family.

The beginning chapters of the book start with some background information on who or what Brahma is and how souls and soul families are set up. We discuss how there are three different types of consciousness that work together to keep us in the state of being alive. We delve briefly into dreams and the possibility of dream realities as well as how memories affect our current reality.

Chapter Four gave me a whole new outlook on reincarnation. Brahma's explanation of how it really works makes far more sense than the popular theories of reincarnation. Chapters Four through Six take us through the experiences of the soul. We hear about the nature of consciousness in all matter, spiritual balance, and love energy. According to Brahma, "*Love is the force that propels the universe.*" We discuss how the choices we make create possibilities and how probabilities are created having their own type of

# Introduction

existence and reality. Brahma also offers an explanation of what happens when our physical bodies separate from our souls at death.

The next three chapters deal with the experience a soul has after death, with opportunities for continuing experience and balancing the physical life's unresolved issues. There is more to learn after death. Brahma explains how relationships are far more important than we generally understand and many spiritual relationships span multiple lifetimes. We also get confirmation that, yes, grandma really is watching and cheering us on in life. According to Brahma we have an entire cheerleading section of passed loved ones, close spiritual guides, and angels watching our experience in life.

The last two chapters offer us insight into how our spiritual evolution has influenced our physical incarnations, and how our evolution might continue. Human life is a grand playground for spiritual experience and we are only partway through the evolution of existence. But human life is not the only kind of incarnation; there are also spiritual entities behind every animal. Certain types of animals are far more spiritually evolved than others. Our relationships with animals are an important part of spiritual and physical existence. Fido and Flipper may be looking to us for compassion, but they have much to teach us and from a spiritual aspect, so we should be looking to them for guidance.

I truly hope you enjoy this material and find it useful. It has helped me immensely with dealing with the deaths of those close to me and continues to offer comfort when I am questioning the circumstances of my life. Having more of an understanding of the nature of our reality makes it easier to be at peace with life's difficulties and heightens the appreciation of its joys.

Introduction

# INTRODUCTION BY BRONWEN SKYE

The night after my brother died I heard his voice in my head. I was lying in bed half awake. He asked me how I was doing, and told me that he was confused. I was relieved to be able to talk with him again, even if it was only in spirit. He said he'd been wandering around a while and wasn't sure what to do. He was only 36 years old and had just, with no precursor or warning, died unexpectedly.

I asked him what happened, why he'd left us so suddenly. He told me it was sort of a spiritual accident. He said he'd meant for the health crisis to be a wake-up call for a change in lifestyle. He'd been a heavy drinker and smoker, albeit a cheerful one, but it was not the healthiest way of living. He said when he got out of his body, it was so enticing that he wanted to stay. He had been gone for so long at that point that brain damage would have occurred had he decided to come back.

I did the only thing I knew how to do at the time; I told him to look for the light. He said thank you, and I let him go. I wished that I could have been more helpful, but I'd had no practice or experience talking to people who had "died" and were now in spirit.

My brother, Paris, was instrumental in helping me with extrasensory experiences. When we were young children, he'd suggest that we meet in a dream. We both loved Herbie the Love Bug, so we often met in that car for our dreams. We would awake and report we'd had the same experiences together the night before.

When I was in college in New York City, Paris had told me about his out-of-body experiences. He said he'd been having them since he was a boy. I was determined to have one myself. I took a class with Rick Stack, a former student of Jane Roberts, one of the preeminent figures in the world of paranormal phenomena, in my quest to do this. I learned the basic tools in class to astrally project. Then the six week class ended, and, though I found myself able to lucid dream, even with consistent practice I was unable to project.

# Introduction

Paris came to visit me one week. He was sleeping on the living room couch during his stay, while I was in my bedroom. One night before he went to sleep, he said he would help me with my projection. He told me to walk down the hall astrally and visit him. I agreed to do this.

That night I tried, as I had been doing faithfully, to project myself out of my body as I drifted off to sleep. I kept trying to float upwards, as I imagined this was how it would happen. Instead, I found myself sinking down into the mattress. This surprised me and it was a bit frightening. I remember scrambling frantically with my spirit hands to climb back up into my body as I sank. Then I realized that if I did not take this opportunity, I would probably be mad at myself for not allowing it. So I just... let go.

I drifted down though the mattress and then out into the darkness of my room. I walked around for a moment, and then remembered my mission to visit my brother. I walked through the doorway and into the hall. I saw some strange looking people sitting there along the corridor. I had forgotten Rick Stack's instructions to will away anything that was not a part of the reality I was trying to connect with. These people disoriented me, so I returned to my room. My eyes immediately snapped open, and I knew I had done it. I shared the experience with my brother who confirmed he had helped me. I didn't ask him how, though I suppose I should have. I guess I always assumed he had these strange powers of a sort.

A week after he died, he spoke to me in my head again. I asked him how he was and he thanked me for my help. He said he'd found the light, and he was now in a very good place.

Two weeks after he died, I really wanted to see him again. I really felt that he might be one of those people who could literally manifest himself in front of me, but I thought I would be too frightened by that, so I asked him to please meet me in a dream. I fell asleep and woke up in my dream on my front steps. The dream was lucid. I knew I was in another reality and not my own, another version of my front door. He came up the walkway. He was wearing rolled up blue jeans like he used to wear in high school, and a pale yellow baseball shirt with baby blue sleeves. He looked younger, as he had in those days, and very healthy.

## Introduction

I was so excited I could barely contain myself. I asked, "Is it really you?" I ran up to him and gave him a hug. I felt the solidness of him and I touched his shoulders and his arms to make sure he was real. I was convinced as I squeezed his solid flesh. He smiled such a beatific smile at me. "It is you, I love you!" I said. He just kept smiling at me, and then said he couldn't stay long, and so I let him go and watched him walk down the driveway, away from me. At home, my eyes snapped open immediately just as they had when I'd had my out of body experience, and I was convinced I'd made contact with my brother.

His death marked a beginning of a journey of deeper spiritual understanding for me. One that resulted in my connecting with what I consider to be my source entity. Did Paris help me with this connection? I find it likely.

A few weeks after Paris died, I had some major dental work done. I was lying in bed recovering, when someone started talking to me in my head. I had not experienced this type of thing before, except when my brother had spoken to me after he died. I remember the voice telling me that the name of my entity was Brahma and that we would be making contact soon. I understood that we all have a greater spiritual entity, a larger entity or higher self that exists, and mine was called Brahma. This gave me a much needed feeling of comfort, and I drifted off to sleep.

When I awoke, I went straight to the computer to look up Brahma to see if there was any record of this name, or if it was unique to me. I was quite disappointed to see that Brahma is the name of a Hindu God of creation. I despondently thought that my entity could certainly not be this Brahma. I now see that this is just another name for God, and Brahma is what I call my personal one. Perhaps my Brahma was trying to convey this to me.

The voice that I spoke to was a female voice and she identified herself as Zillaphia or Zilla for short. Though I was at first disappointed that I couldn't speak to Brahma, this first voice I heard became a fairly consistent companion to me during my recovery. She said she was needed to pave the pathway so that I could speak with Brahma directly. She said I was not yet ready to be able to receive his energy. She was another part of him, a part that it was now easier for me to connect with. She gave me some messages of comfort, and always told me interesting things. Some of them I wrote down, others I did not. She also told me that Brahma was interested in writing a book.

# Introduction

My husband, Robert, was interested in my experiences. He asked me if I could channel these beings I talked with in my head. He said it would be nice to talk with them. I was very nervous, but I agreed to try. I used a meditation to connect, and first, very slowly and cautiously, spoke as Zilla. We recorded these conversations. A few months later I was able to speak as Brahma, who had some very interesting things to say about the souls and consciousness. The chapter names of the book were given to me by Brahma before we began the recordings.

I was surprised by many things. I was surprised at the quality of the content, and also surprised that Brahma expected Robert to be a full partner in helping him flesh out and interpret his ideas, to make them understandable to us. I was surprised by Brahma's obvious humor. As Brahma has said to Robert, "It is a very good use of your philosophy degree." Brahma said this with somewhat of a nod and a wink, because people had always asked Robert, much to his chagrin, what could he possibly do with a philosophy degree.

The following chapters are based on the recorded conversations between Brahma and my husband, Robert.

# CHAPTER 1
## WHO AM I? I AM YOU

This first chapter relates to when I first spoke with Brahma about writing this book. I had spoken with him before in previous sessions but I wasn't sure who he or she was. In this chapter we learn a little about who he represents and his relationship to my wife, Bronwen. We also talk about the structure of families of souls and greater entities as well.

*Good evening.*

Good evening. Am I speaking with Brahma?

*Yes, it is I.*

Hello, it's Robert. Thank you for coming.

*It is always a pleasure.*

Thank you. I'd like to ask a few introductory questions.

*Excellent.*

First of all, I'm trying to understand where it is that you live.

*I live everywhere, and nowhere.*

So when you are coming here to speak, it's just a portion of you, is that correct?

*Yes, that is correct. All of me will not fit.*

Are you a larger part of Bronwen? Are you her greater entity?

*Yes.*

Does that mean greater with respect to other entities or greater or larger than Bronwen?

*I am larger and greater than Bronwen. It is a denser, yet more expansive type of energy. This may seem like a contradiction however, because the energy is more compacted with more information into each particle, if you will. If you were to lay out my compacted particles of energy they would be a greater, larger amount than the energy that makes up Bronwen.*

So can I assume that you are a collection of souls?

*Yes. I have lived many lives.*

Okay. So, if you have lived many lives, does that make you a compilation of lives?

*That is correct.*

So is Bronwen one of your lives?

*Yes, she is a part of me, an offshoot of my energy, created by a spark, a thought of inspiration.*

And you have other lives that you have started from sparks.

*Yes. That is how they tend to begin.*

And then do they live out their own lives and continue on forever, or do they join back with you when they die?

*They continue, but we are always connected and there is always a free flowing energy back and forth between the entity and the spark.*

So do you experience what the people in your lives experience, because of this free flowing energy?

*Yes. I am affected by all of my sparks, as you are affected by your own sparks. They are like grandchildren to me, you see.*

Okay, so your sparks that have become lives, have created more sparks. Correct?

*It continues infinitely, the creation does not cease.*

Okay. So, can these sparks talk to each other?

*Talk may not be quite the right word. They can communicate, but it is not in verbal terms, or in the terms that you normally associate with communication.*

*There is constant energy communication between the sparks of the same entity. You are always affected by your sparks and the sparks of your greater entity, and they are affected by you.*

And these sparks, these different lives, are they occurring simultaneously, or through different periods of time or different places?

*Both. All of the above. It can be 1400 and 2000, at the same time, simultaneously. It is just a storefront, if you will. In a shopping mall, you pass the toy shop and you pass the antique shop and they can exist at the same time. One looks Victorian, for example we will say it is the antique shop; the toy shop looks very modern perhaps, yet they both exist simultaneously. You can go into one shop and experience a Victorian era, or go into the toy shop and experience something more modern.*

And they can be existing at different times.

*But it is the same time. It just looks different. The 1400's are going on as we speak, you see.*

And so, I assume, are the 2500's?

*That is correct.*

(Authors note: I was totally confused at this point, but I wanted to keep the conversation going. The idea of simultaneous time lines is a recurring concept with my conversations with Brahma and is explained more thoroughly in Chapter 4: REINCARNATION).

Okay. I have a few other questions, but I wanted to ask you about a book that Bronwen has been telling me about. It seems as though you are interested in writing a book.

*Yes.*

Is it a book that you want to dictate, that we can then write?

*I will be dictating most of the book. Your help would be appreciated in fleshing out certain areas, and Bronwen can help put it together in a manner that is pleasing to her.*

Okay. Like assembling it?

*Yes, editing and putting things in order, an order that makes sense to her. If it makes sense to her, it will make sense to others.*

Okay. Was this your idea or Bronwen's idea?

*It is done. I was merely giving her a glimpse into the future.*

Ah, okay. Now, she's written down a bunch of different topics to cover [Brahma had earlier related these to her], I guess these are chapters of the book. Are there any that you want to talk about now? Do you want to get started on any in particular?

*Are there any that currently interest you this evening? Your energy is vital to this mix. So if there is something you are leaning towards, it would be best to go there.*

It occurred to me that it would be good to ask the question: Who are you, Brahma? I think the title of this chapter answers "I Am You", but who are you exactly, to put it in your words?

*I am God. I am an entity focused outside of your space and time who can choose to focus within these if I so desire. I am part of you in a sense as well, as we are all part of a greater entity. All entities are connected. And you are getting information from me but it is your experience, so in some sense, I am actually you as I am all of you who choose to hear me. However, I am intimately connected with Bronwen, she is a child of mine, a soul-fragment, but we are all one. Is it clear how you can be talking to me, and be talking to yourself, or is this a concept that needs more explaining?*

I think it needs more explaining. I kind of understand. So we're all part of the same whole, right?

*Yes, we are all a mass of consciousness, of energy.*

But when I talk with a friend of mine, say when I talk with just Bronwen, how is that different than when I talk with you?

*It is not all that different. You are demonstrating that you do have an understanding of this concept. However, I am a greater part. I am Bronwen, but I am more than Bronwen. So when you speak to Bronwen, you are speaking to a smaller part of yourself as well as a smaller part of me. I am also a greater part of you. However, you are more intimately connected to Shalkeera who is a greater part of you. If Bronwen were to speak to Shalkeera, she would, in essence, be speaking to a part of herself that was a little more divorced from her than I am.*

So my greater entity is called Shalkeera?

*Yes. Shalkeera is the name of the greater entity or the collection of souls of which you, Robert, are a smaller part.*

So to describe these relationships in a visual analogy, would it suffice to use an analogy of a tree?

*It might. Please explain.*

I am thinking of a really large tree, and on part of this tree is a big leaf on the end of a branch and I am that big leaf. If you look at the leaf up close you might think that it's an individual. There might also be another leaf nearby on a different branch that is Bronwen. It is also an individual and we are located close to each other, and when the wind blows we are jostled together. We're connected, but only through the whole tree are we physically linked. That would represent how we are spiritually linked.

*Yes, and perhaps Shalkeera is your branch, and Brahma is her branch, and the tree is the whole. That is an excellent analogy.*

And there are many leaves. So in that respect, to carry that analogy further, are you, Brahma, the tree, or part of the tree trunk?

*I am not the trunk. I am a branch, if we use your analogy, that is more connected to the trunk than you or Bronwen are.*

You're a big tree branch, a bigger branch?

*[Humorously] Well if you are a leaf, I need not be very much bigger to be a big branch to you.*

Okay. That helps me understand.

*This analogy should serve to explain it.*

So, were you at one time a small branch?

*Give us a moment. I am small branches now. I am Bronwen and Zilla, and many others. I exist outside of time so I am small and yet large. I am the leaf and the branch and the trunk at the same time. It is a difficult question that you ask because your time and words interfere with explanation. Perhaps you can help me to clarify with your understanding of language.*

Alright, I'll try. Maybe if we can explain it with time and space. Those of us here are always looking at our watches, so to speak, and any event can take a long time. We wait with great anticipation along the lines of time. It's a very big part of our existence.

*Yes.*

This is in contrast to your existence as well as for all those who have passed on. You all live outside of time and physical space, outside of our physical reality. So since there is no physical space where you are like there is in our reality, there is no time where you are. Correct?

*There is no space. And there is all the space in the world. I am trying to answer your question. I was never a leaf because I am many leaves now, and the trunk, and the tree. I extend leaves from my branches to experience being a leaf, and I am Bronwen but I am more than Bronwen, you see. And I am many leaves, but I am the sum of the leaves and the branch.*

Okay.

*I cannot be just a leaf now. I experience leafiness through Bronwen and others. You see, the small comes out of the large. The trunk exists first in this analogy, and then come the branches, and then the leaves.*

Okay. So when Bronwen has an experience, you also benefit from this?

*Yes. I can experience it with her if I choose. But I do not forget who I am or what my perspective is, as she does and as most of you do.*

Okay, so is that how most of your experience is, sort of a vicarious experience through leaves?

*I experience this and my own experiences as well, vicariously, and directly. I can create my own realities and my own problems and challenges, and live in them for a while. I can co-create with other entities. We can create a world, or an environment and interact, and challenge each other, if we choose. Or I can create an environment by myself. Even create other people, if you will, to interact with who only exist within me. But once I create them, they have their own consciousness to do with as they please. But it is all me unless I choose to interact with another branch. However, another branch, in a remote sense, is also me, which is why I am you, which is why we are God. You, and all of us.*

## Who Am I? I Am You

I've heard God referred to as the all-that-is?

*The all-that-is. Yes, indeed, my friend, that is correct.*

So what do you do when you're not talking with us?

*I find things to do, just as you do. You create your own environments and co-create with others in the same way that I do. You are just largely unaware of it. But if you can go through your day aware that you are creating everything, the environment and those that you choose to interact with, it will be somewhat of a different experience for you. You are not the leaf blowing in the wind. You are the leaf connected to the branch. You are strong and you can create, and you do.*

So for example, if Bronwen has an experience, I know you can benefit through that experience. Do you experience everything that she experiences?

*I do, but I can choose not to focus on it if there is something I have enough experience with. Keep in mind, of course, that each experience is unique. Even if I have been to 20 funerals or 200 or 2,000, each funeral will be different and I will benefit in some way. However, I may choose to focus less on one because I have experienced something very similar with a very similar personality fragment. Does this make sense?*

Yes. So a personality fragment is an individual soul?

*Yes, you could consider it to be an incarnate soul.*

Along the lines of personality fragments, I spoke with Zilla or Zillaphia in a previous session.[1] Who is she in relation to you?

*She is another leaf.*

Okay. And there are many others?

*Yes, there are many leaves, many soul-fragments in our tree. Zillaphia is on a different plane of existence than many others, different than Bronwen or you are on. She has passed on, as you say, and has created her own fragment personalities that now exist in worlds similar to your own.*

So she's no longer a leaf, so to speak?

---

[1] **This was the first entity that Bronwen channeled where she spoke as Zillaphia**

*[Humorously] I suppose she is a mini branch, perhaps.*

Okay. But she's connected a little more directly to Bronwen and to you than perhaps, to me. Correct?

*Yes. You have your entity.*

Okay, that helps. I am trying to get at the question that many readers might have: Who is Brahma? Who am I talking to?

*It is very important that people know that they are speaking to themselves when they are speaking to their God. Brahma is a name for God that is used in the East. However, to be clear, I am not this Brahma that they speak of. I am not the Hindu god. Bronwen, as well as the entire entity, tends to like these sorts of sounds, these phonetic names: Bronwen, Brahma, names like this. So this is how we think of ourselves, and this is how it sounds to Bronwen. Someone else experiencing us might not hear the name as Brahma, and might hear it as something different as each experience is unique, and each perspective is different. The sounds that you hear now are not the same types of sounds that I hear. Sound requires no resonance where I come from. It is largely in the mind, you see, and so it can "sound" different. I am not sure if I am making this clear.*

It makes sense in a way if you remember the perspective. Instead of using a specific word or a name for identification, it would be more like if somebody recognizes their friend by their face. Then somebody else might see that same face, but they might not be in agreement about what that face looks like.

*Yes, they might not consider the eyes to be as pretty as the lips.*

Right, some people might focus on different aspects of that face, and that would be the name for them.

*Yes, one person might say: she has a big nose. The other person might say: she's blonde. Yes, like this.*

Or someone would say, that big-nosed girl, or that blonde girl, but they're referring to the same person.

*Yes, exactly. Brahma is the name we have adopted. Although it sounds different to me, even different than it sounds to Bronwen, this is a pleasing name to us, and a pleasing sound within your system, but it is a sound that she associates with us.*

*However, going back to the Eastern religions, I am not that God that they have created, however I am a god nonetheless, and so in some sense, the same. But I do not, as perhaps this other Brahma does, wish for anyone to worship me.*

Okay. Generally speaking, why are you willing to talk to me?

*This information will benefit the world, or whoever touches it, whoever cares to. It will in turn benefit me, and the all-that-is. It is evolutionary and forward-thinking material. It is not entirely new; others before me have said similar things. But refreshment is needed from time to time with this information. People tend to forget and go off on tangents. Now, everyone, of course, is free to believe as they choose. However choosing to believe in this way is a lot more creatively free than in some other ways. And some people are ready for this information so that they can progress more quickly.*

Okay. Well, I am honored you are talking to me; thank you.

*Most certainly, it is my pleasure. You are, of course, as I have said before, instrumental in the making of this text. Your mind is inquisitive and sharp, and the questions and analogies you present will help clarify. There are other teachers that, by themselves, are able to write an entire tome and have the entire world understand it. However, I am a little more removed in some senses than some, and it is good to have someone on this plane to help with clarification. You will fit the bill.*

Thank you. Thank you for coming, and speaking with me.

*Thank you for having me.*

# CHAPTER 2
## THE NATURE OF THE SOUL

In this chapter, we learn more about Brahma's description of the soul and soul families. We get an idea of how a soul coordinates with three different types of consciousness and the physical elements in our physical existence.

*Good evening.*

In our last conversation, we were speaking about souls and soul-fragments. I'd like to get clarification on what we mean when we talk about the soul. There are many ideas about the nature of souls, and I was thinking we could discuss the popular concept of the soul and compare and contrast that with your definition.

*Yes, please explain your view of the common conception of the soul.*

Well, I think the most basic idea is that it is the part of us that possibly lives on when our bodies die. It has been described as incorporeal and immortal. Therefore in popular thinking, it seems to be the part that is created at some time either before our birth or at birth. It is the part of us that makes us tick. It could also be a kind of intelligence since it has something to do with controlling our lives or at least our thinking. It is also commonly used to describe the part of us that thinks or feels emotions or dreams, and is sometimes referred to as our mind or consciousness.

*Yes. And you disagree with this view?*

Well, not entirely, but I guess I am skeptical of it. There seems to be two popular lines of thought here. One is that our consciousness exists as a function of our brain and is only present because we have a physical form. It's the scientific idea that when we are conceived, we ourselves create consciousness with our brains and the mind and soul are tied together in the brain.

*Yes the scientific Darwinian view of reality or consciousness.*

This view implies that consciousness is a thing that simply resides in our physical bodies. And when we die or the body dies, the cells die and therefore the consciousness dies with it and can no longer exist. The soul dies.

*Indeed.*

The other line of thought is the typically spiritual aspect of it where God created the soul and the soul is somehow attached to an embryo, and then there's a birth and there's a life with a body connected to the soul, and if that soul lives somehow in touch with a God, it continues on after death. When the body dies the soul goes to heaven or possibly to hell.

*Well neither view is 100% incorrect. There are kernels of truth in both views, however neither view embraces or sees the entire picture.*

Right. I suspected that.

*It is true that your cells have a consciousness of their own that will stay when you die, meaning they do not come with you. The cells of the brain are an example of this. Your mind goes with you, but not your brain. And of course on the religious side one could say there is a god that creates you. Remember, however, that god is YOU. The omniscient presence is not something outside of your self. It is with you in this life and with you as you depart from it.*

Okay, so, how is it related to consciousness? If the cells have a consciousness and the brain has a consciousness, what role does the soul play in consciousness?

*The soul is a kind of energy which is seeking expansion. It is a student, the brightest student in the class, the one whose nature is to learn. It is hungry for knowledge. The soul, this intelligence, is a consciousness in and of itself. It gives birth to other consciousness, and when a part of your soul or consciousness incarnates in this realm, other consciousness is attracted to it.*

*These things on the earthly plane have consciousness of their own. A blade of grass or anything that makes up the earth—a cell or a molecule—is attracted to your soul, which you send forth to incarnate, and in unison there is an agreement. The earthly elements create your body and they live within your body. It is your soul consciousness and the consciousness of the physical elements combined that create your earthly experience.*

*If you can recall, when you are in the dream state you will find there is no consciousness communicating with you from, say, your fingertip. You will not feel it because it is not with you. It is a body consciousness which, if I can explain this clearly, has its own consciousness as a conglomeration of cells. So there is the consciousness of the individual cells and then a body consciousness, which you also do not take with you in dreams, or after what you like to call the death experience. We would like you to help us clarify.*

Okay. So the soul is not necessarily consciousness, it's sort of helped by consciousness?

*It is intelligence and it is conscious intelligence, so in this sense it is consciousness. It just is not the entire consciousness that you experience. I must also point out that the individual cells in your body come and go. They die like you die. But the main consciousness of the body that unites them creates an experience of continuation so you do not notice when individual cells die because of the unifying body consciousness.*

Okay, like the skin cells that flake off and are replaced with new ones.

*Yes, they are little consciousnesses that agreed to become part of your experience for a time, and that agreed to help you in return for being part of you.*

Right. But I don't feel like I'm missing anything when they go.

*Not unless you take off a large chunk of your arm.*

Yes, then I would definitely feel like I'm missing something.

*Yes.*

So there are different types of consciousness. There is a smaller, cellular consciousness that resides in individual cells or molecules of our bodies and there is a body consciousness that controls these cells and the more complex systems of the body.

*Yes, and there is also the consciousness of what you think of as the soul that is always with you: in the dream state, in your waking life, and beyond these states as well. But it is, if you will notice, of a different clarity, it is not quite the same. You do not use your brain when you are in your dreams. You use your mind. There are things which you are used to doing with your brain consciousness that you cannot do in the dream state. Reading and math seem to be somewhat problematic at times during this state because that is somewhat a function of the brain. The soul or spirit consciousness does not need to read or do math. It simply has a knowing of things. If you would like to read a book and you are not connected to a body you can just experience it and know it. You do not have to read the words. The soul is a mind consciousness.*

Okay. That would have been helpful in college. Skipping the reading that is. Not the part about not being connected to a body.

*Indeed!*

So we have at least three types of consciousness: Molecular consciousness, body consciousness, and mind consciousness.

*Yes, that is correct.*

So how is it then that the soul is attached to our bodies? Maybe it is the other way around as you are saying that the parts of the body, the cellular consciousnesses, are attracted to the soul.

*Yes, they are created in concert with the soul. They agree to be a part of you for a time. They are a part of you yet they have their own consciousness. This is similar to Bronwen having her own consciousness separate from me. She is a part of me but she has her own consciousness. However, she did not create the basic molecules of the cells in her body. These molecules from Earth are of Earth consciousness and chose to participate in the corporeal consciousness. The consciousness of the molecules of Earth that make up her cells chose to work with her. So although I created her I did not create her cells. She is working with them in concert with her soul and consciousness and, of course, me.*

Okay.

*Does this make sense?*

Yes, kind of. So the soul is just sort of the leader of a group?

*Yes, one could say that. The group being the body and the cells and molecules that make up the body. You are made up of many consciousnesses. You are primarily aware of two: the body consciousness and the consciousness of your mind. You are aware of your mind consciousness and can feel your body consciousness. Similarly, a tree can feel its leaves and, although leaves can fall off of the tree as they do each year in the fall in some areas of the world, the tree still lives on and still experiences.*

So then, the body consciousness would be in charge of bodily functions and those things I may or may not always be aware of such as breathing and digesting and healing.

*That is correct.*

This is not the same as the mind or soul consciousness. When I am dreaming and I wake up and I remember my dream, the part of me that was dreaming, that was experiencing the dream, is my mind consciousness. Correct?

*Yes. For practical purposes we will say yes.*

It obviously is not my physical body.

*And it is not the entire you. But yes, for purposes of this conversation that is your soul or mind consciousness.*

Dreaming and death are soul or mind consciousness experiences that involve separation from the body. Can we call this ability to separate from the physical realm a characteristic of the nature of the soul?

*The nature of the soul is to expand and to learn. It is not a thing. It is a way of being. Do you see? Something's nature is how it is, generally. One of your cats has a sweet nature. Another cat has an ornery nature. The nature of the soul is that of an avid student. It wishes to expand and to grow. It is always seeking evolution. It seeks in as many corners of experience as it can find. Your soul seeks not only in the earthly realm and the realm of dreams but seeks in other realms that you are largely unaware of in this life, though you may sometimes encounter them in your dreams.*

*It is you. It is energy. It is intelligence. It is hunger for knowledge.*

Okay. So, the soul obviously does not have a physical aspect; it is just focused here in this reality. Right? My soul is focused with my body and this physical reality most of the time. Correct?

*Well, I would not necessarily say most of the time. I would say* some *of the time.*

Some of the time? Does that mean that some of the time the soul is focused elsewhere?

*Yes.*

Where?

*In other realms of experience or perhaps in other fragments of your entity family of selves. But you see, we must be careful to differentiate; are you speaking of Robert or Shalkeera?* [2]

Yes, that is a good question. I guess I'm speaking of Robert, my personality fragment. I think that is the way most people here consider themselves, as a singular soul.

*A soul seemingly unattached to something larger.*

Yes, the thing that we can't see that is controlling our bodies and actions.

*Then, in that case, most of the time you are focused here. Some of the time you are focused in your dreams and some of the time you are focused in areas that you are largely unaware of because you are not able to interpret it into your earthly experience. However, when you go to a dreaming state you can sometimes glimpse these areas.*

So my soul that is largely focused in Robert is just a small part of my larger entity?

*Yes.*

We are using the word 'entity' as being the larger collection.

*Yes, the larger collection from whence you came that is largely, although not entirely, an entity in and of itself. Meaning of course, it sprang from something else but it is enough of a solo collection as to be considered your entity. Does this make sense?*

Yes.

*Good.*

---

[2] It seems that when Brahma refers to us as "all one", it is because he seems to always look at us as a conglomerate entity. This, I suspect, is due to his perspective. His self-concept is a conglomeration and he sees everyone that way. From his perspective, that is how we are.

In my case it is the Robert family along with his Shalkeera family entity? But that's different from say, Bronwen's family entity.

*Yes. Although, our entities are similar in nature and so it is easy for us to coalesce and experience and together learn from each other. Sort of like you and Bronwen are both Americans of a similar age, you see. You come from a similar background and you have had similar experiences growing up even though they were not the same experiences or even in the same cities. And so our entities are like that.*

So, can we use the term larger soul interchangeably with the word entity?

*Semantics are difficult. But if you would like for us to establish a language we can do this if it would make things easier.*

Yes. I think it would.

*The soul is a consciousness from a consciousness. The entity I am referring to is an umbrella for [the sum total of] all of your consciousness and consciousness fragments. The soul is the entity and also the fragment. Would it be helpful if we refer to them as fragments?*

Yes. Soul-fragments.

*Yes. I do not wish to diminish you or your experience by calling you a fragment, however.*

Right. But that's what it is, a piece of a larger whole?

*Yes. Then in this case, yes, we may use entity and larger soul interchangeably.*

So we will refer to the larger soul as the larger entity which is a collection of soul-fragments or individuals. Also, we have the personality fragment which is a soul incarnate where we also have three types of consciousness: the mind consciousness, the body consciousness, and the molecular consciousness that are attached to a particular soul-fragment in this physical life.

*Yes, in your case your soul, your larger self, your larger entity is Shalkeera. What you refer to as Robert is your soul-fragment which is your sense of individuality. Your earthly experience is an orchestration of your mind or soul consciousness with your body consciousness and molecular consciousnesses. Your body consciousness helps your brain analyze things and it also governs your bodily functions of digestion, healing,* and breathing among others. The molecular consciousness is smaller and exists in the food you eat, the individual cells in your body, and in all of nature on Earth.

Okay. So then, the act of thinking would be sort of a mind consciousness process, either with or without the assistance of the brain?

*Yes.*

What about emotions and passion or ambition?

*These can be caused by body consciousness but they are largely a function of the larger consciousness of the entity. Not that passion is necessarily of the entity, but the power that fuels the passion is of the entity.*

Okay. So in this case we are referring to passion not as the desire, but as the motivation behind the desire?

*It is the energy behind it. The ability to do it. The strength for the expression. If your body consciousness is angry, to express this anger it needs energy. It needs a force to get it out. This force is lovingly provided by your entity who sees a need and fills it. You have a need to express this anger that you feel you may have come by in your earthly experience, and your entity provides the power for expression.*

So emotions are fueled by the larger entity.

*Yes.*

Now, the title of our chapter is the Nature of the Soul. You mentioned a hunger for knowledge and expansion. Can you help me understand the goal or purpose of the soul?

*Yes, it desires to evolve, to learn, to understand, to know itself more with every creation of every soul-fragment. With every experience it gets its fingers into it evolves and becomes larger and more expansive. The entity wishes to experience as many things as it can think of and it would seem, as of yet, there is a never ending supply of things it can think of to experience. And so the expansion continues.*

Through experience?

*Yes. Through thinking of things and then experiencing them. For example, an entity might say, "I wonder what it would be like to be a small white rat and to live under a floorboard," and voilà, a part of the entity experiences this. There are hundreds of billions of things that can be thought of in terms of experience. I'm using hundreds of billions of course lightly, it is in truth many more than that.*

You might be using hundreds of billions because it is a sufficiently large number for our imaginations.

*For you to understand. Indeed. But as of yet there have been no entities that have said, "Oh, that's it, I've experienced everything. I quit." That has not yet happened. There is always a new angle for even a similar experience, you see. "What if I was an actress who lived in America?" Or "What if I was an actress who lived in France?" Or "What if I was an actress who lived in France in 1940? Or "What if I was an actress who lived in France in 1842?" You see, there are so many variations, so many things you can think of to experience on just one theme.*

Yes. So then does the soul provide the motivation for our experience?

*Yes, the soul by nature is motivated, as you say, which is a lovely description.*

So, the feeling I get when I'm doing something that I'm really into, that passion, that flow of creativity, is that coming from the soul?

*Yes, you are experiencing it rather than thinking about it. Rather than using your brain you are more connected to this soul energy. And therefore you can understand it more clearly on an intuitive level.*

And that's because of the soul? The feeling I get when I feel like I have the energy and enthusiasm and excitement about something is from the soul?

*That is due to your tapping into soul energy.*

Tapping into soul energy?

*Yes.*

So does it follow then when I'm just tired and unmotivated I am not getting any soul energy?

*A trickle perhaps. It probably means that you are not tuned in very well and you are experiencing your body consciousness but not very much of your soul. In this case you may need to reconnect. Meditation or a nap or something else will be helpful.*

Okay. Just a couple more soul questions. I've read that certain people, philosophers, have had a tendency to define the soul in terms of separating it out into different parts. For example an emotional aspect, a mind aspect, and more of a physical, moving aspect. Is that accurate?

*One can think of it in this way. However, it is all connected. The intelligence and emotion, though slightly different in nature, are inextricably connected to the soul. They cannot be pulled apart. However, the energy of the body or the consciousness of the body can be separated from the soul, but only in the death experience or when you are dreaming. So if you would like, because of the different natures of these types of consciousness, you can separate it if that makes it easier for you to understand. However, as I said, these things, especially intelligence and emotion within the soul, cannot be pulled apart.*

Okay.

*You are whole and complete.*

Yes. So, what about when a soul-fragment has the death experience or passes on? What happens to the body consciousness? I'm speaking of the molecular consciousness that exists in the cells as well. For example, the part that heals the cut on your finger, that runs the body and the bodily functions, the part that grows your toenails. What do these consciousnesses do when the soul leaves? Is that the correct phrase to use? The soul leaves? Does it go somewhere else?

*The soul is reabsorbed back within the larger entity. However, of course, it retains its own individual consciousness.*

We like to say here that the soul leaves as if it has a physical location.

*Which of course it does not. You will find yourself retreating inward and joining a family of familiar energy when you choose to depart. Your cells will die, and their consciousnesses will go to other places on the planet. They may find their way to someone else who has an incarnation, or they may go to a rock or a tree or water. The consciousnesses will simply turn their attention somewhere else. They will scatter because they are all individual. The body consciousness, however, will, in a sense, die. This is what we can think of as the ego. And it knows there is a death of sorts for it. So this makes it scary. It does not want to let go. You might call it survival instinct.*

Okay, so can we talk about this ego?

*Yes.*

What do you mean when you use the word "ego"? What is the ego in this sense?

*It is a construct that your consciousness creates in order to help you integrate with the consciousness of the earth that created your body. It is necessary to hold it together while you are experiencing this form of reality. It is somewhat of an artificial construct in that it thinks it lives in the only reality. It has a kind of narrow focus or concept of its own reality. However, this is somewhat necessary in order to navigate on this earthly plane of existence. It is complicated.*

Perhaps we can use an analogy to clarify. I'm seeing the ego as being like a building contractor. When you want to build a house you hire a contractor. The contractor deals with the plumber and electrician and the carpenter and coordinates everyone needed to complete the project.

*Yes, that is a very nice analogy.*

Because I don't know how to deal with all of these specialized house builders, the contractor deals with them. And so you are saying that for the contractor, the ego, to operate most effectively, the contractor needs to believe he is running everything.

*Yes. He needs to believe he is running the show. And therefore when he feels threatened, he becomes fearful. Some people do not even like to remember their dreams because the ego is so threatened by this. However of course, one can stretch the ego if one learns to accept these things, and the ego will see that it does not necessarily have to die a horrible death in order to grow. There is death for it in a sense at the departing. But a part of that will also be reabsorbed within the entity. But you see, it does not continue in an individual consciousness like you do. It is sort of a prop man, you see. It is there temporarily, whereas you exist forever.*

Okay. Because without me the contractor wouldn't have a job.

*This is correct and it no longer has a job when you leave the earthly reality.*

When I tell him the job is done. When I die.

*Yes. It is part of you. But it is reabsorbed. Although as I said, this is a different kind of re-absorption than you going back to your entity because the individuality of you is not lost. The contractor is somewhat lost although could be called upon again if needed.*

In a new life?

*Yes.*

So there could be similar egos among different lives of the same entity?

*Yes.*

That would explain physical similarities among personality fragments when there is reincarnation. Is that helpful in dealing with earthly things?

*Yes. The ego is a tool. It has its own consciousness of sorts, but it is not you and it is not as important as you.*

Okay.

*But it becomes very excited on the earthly plane and likes to take over. It has not been entirely perfected by creative entities, if you can understand this. Entities are still working on a better ego. There are issues and problems. For example, it was not intended to disconnect you so completely from your soul and others as it often does.*

Yes, so that is just sort of a side effect of being so effective?

*Yes, exactly. And we have not come up with a perfect design. But there is no perfection, there is only growth. So we will grow and we will perhaps find something better.*

Okay.

*But for now this is what works. It is the best that we have found.*

Okay. Let me make sure I understand you so far.

*Would you like to try to explain your understanding?*

Good idea. My understanding of the soul is that it is sort of the energy or the part of an entity who is created or fragmented; as they say here: it is a chip off the old block. It resides in the body but only because it has created the body. It has assembled the elements and compounds and the physical things of this earth into a body using the consciousness that resides in all of the earthly elements.

*And the Earth is a consciousness in and of itself consisting of lots of small [forms of] consciousness. In this respect it is like an entity.*

Okay, you are referring to all the physical matter, basically?

*Yes, and collectively it has a consciousness like yours though different in some ways.*

Right. And so the soul has assembled all these consciousness forms together.

*With their agreement.*

With their agreement, and in unison they operate as a living being.

*Yes.*

These consciousness forms are giving information back and forth with each other and with the ego and the soul consciousness. This provides feedback and information for our senses. And the soul, being the receiver of all of this, is the facilitator of this cooperative venture. The soul is doing all of this out of the motivation that it desires to grow and expand and evolve through experience, and it can better achieve that experience in this earthly realm through the use of this body and this wonderful cooperation of all our forms of consciousness.

*Yes.*

Furthermore, spiritually, we all gain from this experience. And the driving factor is primarily the soul-fragment, which is part of the larger entity.

*Yes, but the entity is also the driving factor.*

But the part that's running the body is the soul-fragment?

*Yes. Yes it is a soul-fragment from a larger over-soul, shall we say.*

And the soul-fragment is not only working with this body but it is dabbling in other realities and experiencing other experiences through imagination or whatever during dreams or daydreams or night dreams and this soul-fragment continues on after the death experience.

*I would like to say, have no fear, you will know yourself when you die. You will still be you.*

Because I will be reabsorbed back into the entity.

*Yet you will have your individual consciousness. The re-absorption is like a coming home party. It is a celebration and it is a comforting feeling of togetherness. Yet you are you and you are your own individual so your personality will not be lost.*

Okay, so it is not so much a re-absorption.

*Perhaps that is not the word that is best used in this case.*

Maybe a reunion.

*A reunion is a very nice word for this.*

---

Okay. So, Brahma is a collection of soul-fragments, a larger entity. Correct?

*Yes.*

And Bronwen is a soul-fragment?

*Yes. Who can also become a collection as well.*

Now, in our conversations it seems as though we have talked a lot about Brahma and Shalkeera being sort of collections of soul-fragments or groups of souls.

*Yes, sort of like an over-soul or a larger soul encompassing all the smaller souls. It is larger than you. You sprang from it. It would be the ocean to the raindrop that is you.*

Okay, so is Brahma larger than Shalkeera?

*No.*

Shalkeera is larger than Brahma?

*We think perhaps a little bit, though we do not generally think in these terms.*

Okay. Now, Bronwen can also become a collection of soul-fragments, but she is of your creation. Correct?

*Yes.*

I think very highly of her. She is amazingly smart and highly sensitive and is anything but a simple creation from a simple soul.

*Why thank you.*

Is she a direct creation of yours?

*Yes, a direct creation.*

So she is not a soul-fragment created from a soul-fragment that was a creation of yours?

*That is correct. She is her own new creation. There were bits of my energy, you see, that wished to be Bronwen, which had this inkling of a type of person, a type of incarnation to be. And so, with my careful thought and planning and the energy's own impetus, Bronwen sprang into creation.*

Okay.

*The energy had certain tendencies you see, to become a certain way, and I helped it to form.*

Okay. I mean, obviously she doesn't seem that she was just a spur of the moment creation from a smaller or more simple soul-fragment.

*No, this was a careful planning. This was not an accidental thought, though it is good to see that you understand that this can happen.*

Wait, so are there really people that I run into on the street that are just that— accidental creations?

*Yes. You can sometimes tell because they don't seem quite all there. They don't seem to quite understand how to get on in the world. They seem to be lacking depth. They need to fill out. They are not yet fully formed.*

Do you mean they are childlike?

*Yes, in some ways.*

Even as adults?

*That is correct. And conversely, some children can be spotted as careful creations because they seem to be what you call old souls. When, of course, the truth is they are FROM old souls who have carefully planned them. They carry the energy of that soul as Bronwen carries my energy. Similarly, you carry Shalkeera's energy, who is also not a young entity.*

So there are soul-fragments like the people I see each day. And these are part of larger families of souls called entities.

*Yes, that is correct.*

And every soul or soul-fragment can create the spark of a new soul?

*Yes. The spark of a new soul can be created by larger entities or newer soul-fragments. The power of creation is inherent in the energy of the universe. Each soul-fragment has the potential to grow and expand, though the amount of expansion and growth can vary considerably.*

# CHAPTER 3
## DREAMS

In this discussion on dreams, Brahma and I talk about the value and about the meaning of dreams, especially how they can be influenced by other personalities in a larger entity family. The discussion also sheds some light on the nature of memories.

---

*Good evening.*

Good evening, Brahma. Dreams have been on my mind lately. Can we talk a little bit about dreams and how they relate to the soul?

*Very well then.*

Can you tell me what dreams are?

*Dreams are manifestations of your awareness. They are a part of you as much as you are a part of this earth. They are your recharging station and they are also your "jumping off" station as well. When you slip into a dream, part of you is in physical reality and a larger part of you is in this mysterious dreamland. It is not just one land however, but is many lands. You have experienced this by going to many different locations in your dreams.*

*When you dream you are not only recharging your physical life energy, but you are also dispersing ideas that you have had throughout the day. You are sending them to other portions of the entity. You are playing with them, and you are experiencing them. You are trying them out to see if they would be helpful for you to experience in this physical reality or some other type of reality that you might be simultaneously involved in.*

So in regard to dreams, I understand a lot of them are based on the experiences I've had, that day, for example. Then, at other times, I have no idea where they're coming from. They seem like they have nothing to do with what I have recently experienced and sometimes nothing to do with me. Are they some form of experience that another related spark of my entity may be having?

*Yes. Very good, my friend. These are communications from off-shoots of your personality and off-shoots of your entity. You may often have dreams that seem like they are "out of left field". For instance, you may dream you were a baseball player. You would think it was very strange for you to be a baseball player in a dream if you have no great love of sports. But you do have personalities who are interested in such things, and therefore you may dream of these other ideas that come from different personalities that are a part of you. And you help them play out their creations, as they help you play out yours.*

*In dream realities sometimes the personality in question is not at liberty to fulfill a creation, but it must be fulfilled in some way, so sometimes you will take on this task for them, or for you, as they are part of you. It helps the whole entity, you see. What helps one, helps all. Sometimes, personalities are unable to get the connection they need, the rest they need, the deep sleep that they need, and so sometimes they cannot play these creations out. Sometimes you are requested, and you fulfill these of your own free will. If you can learn, in your dreams, to catch yourself doing something very strange, you can have more of a communication with the personality you are assisting.*

So if I notice that I'm playing baseball, for example, then that would be a clue to me to know that I'm communicating with another personality that is into baseball. Correct?

*Yes, another personality that is related to you. You could then perhaps communicate on a more immediate level if you were aware of this. But when you are dreaming, you do not bring your conscious mind with you very often, and so these things do not occur to you. Usually, it is just happening. It is second nature and you do not think of it. But if you bring the conscious mind with you into the equation when you are dreaming, you will be able to figure more things out, and you could consciously connect with this other personality.*

Now if I'm experiencing a dream based on an experience that another personality is having, is that a dream of what they're dreaming? Or is that a dream of what they are living? Are they really playing baseball, or are they dreaming about playing baseball?

*They may be playing baseball, but more likely, they have a creative desire which needs be fulfilled in an idea of baseball. For instance, if a personality lives in the city, near no fresh fields of grass or baseball diamonds, but has a great love of baseball, perhaps, if this person cannot play baseball himself or even dream of baseball, then perhaps you could do it for him, and fulfill this creative need in some small way. Now, when you fulfill this creative need for him, it may satisfy him enough that he continues to live happily in the city, or it may inspire him to move to the country where he can actually play baseball. The creation can lead to many different avenues for a personality, whether you fulfill the creation or the personalities fulfill it themselves. You can of course always fulfill these creative desires in physical life outside of dreams, but sometimes that option is not always immediately available.*

So if somebody has a creative need that needs to be fulfilled, and say it is a desire to play baseball, then that is a creation that needs to happen. So how is *my* dreaming a kind of creation for him?

*You are also creating in your dreams. You are fulfilling and creating at the same time, if you can imagine such a thing to be possible.*

So I'm fulfilling their creative need by satisfying their desire to play baseball and I'm doing this by playing it out in my dreams?

*Playing it out in your own way, which will be a different way, perhaps, than the personality itself would have played it out. But the personality will gain something from your insight, from your originality, from your particular way of playing out this creation, and will perhaps see it in a new light.*

I find that interesting, I guess I hadn't really thought of dreams as being creative in their own right.

*Indeed, you can create new worlds in dreams if you choose. Every dream is not like every other dream. In other words, every dream is not always a fulfillment of a creation, or a casting off of various ideas that you have had in the physical world during the week. Sometimes, it is pure creation for creation's sake. Bronwen sometimes has dreams of amusement parks, and she is very creative in these. She creates rides, and attractions and worlds that are very interesting to her. This is a fun exercise, which also literally creates a world that she can come back to or not.*

*Part of herself will always reside in these places, and the world she created will continue on with or without her attention.*

So this type of dream is not just a creative idea that she should build an amusement park. It is creative in its own right. Correct?

*Yes, sometimes they are creative in their own right. Creation for the sake of creation, for the sake of fun, perhaps.*

So it's also a form of expression.

*As all life is, yes.*

What about frightening dreams or frustrating dreams or even nightmares that people have?

*There can be several reasons for a frightening dream. One can be that another personality that is so bothered by a thing that it reaches all segments of the entity. Another can be a lowering of vibration, and if fear is encountered on any level in the subconscious, it can be expressed through a nightmare. Or sometimes one will take his or her own negativity and turn it into something that they can fight or conquer. And it is an attempt to resolve the issue.*

That makes sense because then they could conquer the fear, which could then change their feelings about it, which could actually change their reality if they have a different feeling about it.

*If they change their feelings, their reality will change. They can create a scary monster to chase them, and if they vanquish the monster or embrace the monster, they can let go of the fear in the physical and in other realms as well. Sometimes it is helpful, for a personality who is less strong to have someone who is stronger play out a fear for them. Ultimately they will need to experience some of it themselves, but if another segment of the personality experiences the fear for them, it teaches them how to deal with it. They may have a better way, a more immediate way. Sometimes this sort of thing is a cry for help. A personality may cry for help among all personalities or soul-fragments in the entity; it sends out this spark of feeling through the whole entity and some of the personalities will have frightening dreams because of it. Now if your vibration is high enough, you will not perceive the fright.*

What do you mean by vibration?

*The vibration or frequency of the energy of the personality affects all experiences. The higher the vibration, the more joy and love one feels; lower vibrations are accompanied by feelings of disappointment, fear, grief. Everyone's mood changes but some people have tendencies to stay at certain levels. Of course, I would recommend trying to stay at a higher vibration as much as possible.*

So the perception of the fear is influenced by the vibration of the personality?

*Yes. So if your vibration or current emotional state is similar, you will be affected similarly by such a thing. The personality can send sparks throughout the whole entity, and all will experience it on some level, but those with the higher vibration will not really notice it unless they purposefully wish to help.*

Okay.

---

I write down a lot of my dreams, at least pieces of them, and when I'm rereading them sometimes I don't really see much of the meaning. Are there things I should look for to try to find meaning in my dreams, or are a lot of them just creative expressions?

*There is meaning in all of your dreams, but sometimes they are just creative expressions. Perhaps you should try to figure out whether they were just a creative flash for your own enjoyment or they were trying to solve something, or perhaps you could intuitively decide that they were coming from another personality.*

If dreams can be sort of a communication with other personalities who are close to me, if I chose to, could I experience more dreams with this baseball player, for example?

*Yes, you can consciously tell yourself before you sleep that you will meet the baseball player in your dreams. Now of course the trick is to remember the dream of the baseball player after you awaken. If you are writing your dreams down, this is of great assistance because you will remember at least some of your dreams. So yes, you can meet people again in your dreams. You must think of them before you retire. Your thought will call to them, and since you cannot meet them in this physical reality that you have created, then that will be the only way they can answer you: in* the other dream reality. Although I do not want to mislead you; the dream reality is not one reality, but many. However, the channels are much more open there than in this physical realm.

So all these other personalities, are they necessarily living lives that are different from mine in different places and different times? Or is it possible that I've actually met some of them?

*It is possible for this to happen, but not very likely. Most of the time when you have two personalities that are very similar, and wish to go to the same time and experience a similar set of circumstances, although no set of circumstances or time will be exactly like another one, usually when this similarity of desire occurs, you will be split off into two separate physical realities that may overlap slightly but are not the same. They would be just enough away that you will never run into this person, for the most part.*

So I shouldn't be watching out for people at work that are close personalities, because it's unlikely there will be any?

*It is unlikely that it is from the direct entity from which you sprang. However, if you go further back in your entity ancestry, there can be others who are kin to you from your great, great entity, if you will. So you can run into personalities who are a little bit further removed who are still part of your greater entity family and therefore part of you in some sense.*

Is there anything that you specifically think we should know about dreams that we don't understand?

*It would behoove you to try to bring your consciousness into your dreamland. This will make your transition much easier [when you go] from what you call death into a state that is less familiar to you. You will bring some of your conscious mind with you when you die. You do not often do this when you dream. It is a similar sensation. So if you can learn to be conscious in your dreams, you will be more comfortable with that feeling when your transition occurs. And you will be more adept at working in the dream environment since you will not just leave your conscious mind behind like an old blanket that you toss away. So if you learn to manipulate in the dream world while you are still in physical, it will help you later on.*

Is this what people call lucid dreaming?

*Yes. By bringing part of your mind consciousness into your dreams, you will achieve more of an awareness of the dream within the dream.*

So how can I practice bringing my conscious mind into my dreams?

*You need to suggest to yourself before you sleep at night that you will become conscious in your dreams. You need to notice anything that is unusual in your dreams, like purple flying elephants. Now many times in your dreams you let these things go, and you decide that this is just another normal, purple, flying elephant. But if you saw one in your waking life, you would be very surprised.*

Yes.

*So you need to look for these inconsistencies, and when you see these inconsistencies, you will know that you are dreaming. Now it makes it even better if you can look for inconsistencies during the day, because this will get you into the habit of looking for inconsistencies. You look around you periodically during the day and you say, "Is my reality as it should be? Is everything happening as it usually does? Does everything fall into the requirements of physical reality?" And if it does, you look around you with a discerning critical eye and you say, "All right, I'm not dreaming." But if you look around and your cat is standing on his head in some strange yoga pose, you might say, "Well that is unusual, perhaps I am dreaming", and begin to critically look at other things in your environment that might also not match.*

Then if I can recognize that, then I can pull my conscious mind into my dream?

*Yes, it is the trick of pulling your conscious mind in. That is very well put.*

If I have my conscious mind in my dreams, then that opens up the possibility of a bigger experience?

*Yes, it is possible for you to do much more if you can do this, and it is much more thrilling. You will wake up more energized, and you will have greater problem-solving abilities in your physical life if you learn to manipulate your dreams with your conscious mind. The field of dreaming is so creative that you cannot help but bring some of it back. You bring your conscious mind with you into the dreams and you solve all these problems. When you awake you feel there is no problem you can't solve because you have already solved it in a dream. Now, in the dream it seems easier because you can instantly create whatever it is you want. You can create whatever you think about. There is no time delay in the dream state as there is in physical reality, but you will have a more intuitive grasp of how it works. Therefore you will be able to intuitively solve problems in the physical reality.*

---

Now, why do I forget my dreams? Why do I wake up and try to think about my dream but I can't remember it?

*You are too involved in the physical, as most of you are. Everything that you can see and hear and touch is of utmost importance to you. You give very little importance to the inner workings of what is behind the mask of the physical. So you pay it not much mind, it is not as important to you as what you're going to eat for breakfast, or who you're going to be talking to that day, or how much money you have in the bank.*

So is it like I'm not really paying much attention to my dreams? Like when you have a class, for example, and you're not really paying attention to the teacher, and you don't really hear what the teacher says? Is that why I can't remember, the same reason I can't remember what the instructor said?

*That is correct, you are not giving it due importance or paying attention, and you are in the habit of doing that. It also has to do with not bringing your conscious mind with you because if your conscious mind awakes in a dream, you will retain that dream.*

I have one burning question, and it has to do with remembering dreams, maybe it's a question about memories in general. Why is it that there are things I've been able to remember, and then later on, I remember having known them at one time, but I can no longer actually remember them, like I've forgotten something? For example I know I used to be able to recite a particular poem and now the lines escape me. Is that knowledge that's lost, or experience that's lost? Can I recover that?

*You can recover it if you choose. However, very often, as in this case, you have stepped into a different time-space reality. You are a slightly different evolvement at this time. There is Robert of ten minutes ago, and there is Robert of now. The Robert of ten minutes ago may be the Robert of now, or he may not be. He may have changed significantly in the last ten minutes having seen a wondrous or horrifying sight. You might be a different personality at that point. For example, there are photos of you from your past that you do not appreciate today. These pictures are not of you. They are of someone who you were, but you have evolved from this person and you are no longer that person, you see. You are not the same. That person continued on, doing different things, it is not you.*

So when I make the transition, when I die, would I have access to all of these memories?

*Yes. You would have access to any memories that you cared to have access to.*

So they don't go away?

*No, they are retained.*

They can be served up if I need them?

*Yes, nothing is ever lost.*

That's good to know. So when I can't really remember something that I'm trying to remember, it's because I've changed.

*Sometimes it is because you are a different personality at that point.*

But I'm close enough to being the same that it bugs me that I can't remember.

*Yes. You were a different person ten minutes ago, but now you are not this person and you may have trouble reaching back.*

But experiences are never lost even though I can't always remember them?

*Experiences are never lost. You will be able to recall any experiences you wish to, after you have made the transition from this life to your next state of consciousness.*

And possibly here under the right circumstances?

*Certainly, if you have a desire to remember.*

So all those classes I took in college are not wasted?

*You grew from those classes in ways that you do not even remember. They made you who you are; they shaped you and formed you in some way.*

I guess they did.

*They are in your vibrational code, even if you do not remember them.*

That's good to know because I was wondering where they went. It seems like there are a lot of things I can't remember. Would that be an indicator that I've changed a lot?

*Yes, more often than not. If you are young, and you still are, very often it is because you have changed quite a lot. Now, if you are getting older, perhaps you are starting to make your transition early. This is sometimes referred to as Alzheimer's. You can start to move out, you see, before you're actually moved out. You can start packing your metaphorical boxes and moving them somewhere else.*

That would be when people are old and they're getting close to death and are losing their memory?

*Yes. They go back and forth between that reality and this reality because they're not really sure they want to experience the transition, but they don't really know if they want to stay, and so they are sort of in a state of flux.*

Now, if those people had been practicing bringing their consciousness into their dreams, would they still be having this indecision problem?

*They may not be. It is so beneficial to do this. I cannot stress this enough. You would be head and shoulders above any of your peers, so to speak. You would have a very huge leg up were you to do this on a somewhat regular basis at least.*

You mean bringing my consciousness into the dreams?

*Yes. Dream reality operates in a very similar way to the reality you will experience when you transition, or die.*

Would meditation be a bit of a practice as well?

*Meditation is good because it takes your focus out of the physical world and brings it inward, and this in turn reinforces the importance of the inner world, which is what you all so often ignore. Placing importance on this will give you more experience of it. More experience with it will make you more adept at exploring.*

# DREAMS

What happens when you don't dream enough, when you don't get enough sleep?

*A human can go insane from this. Surely you have read about this phenomenon.*

Yes. Why is it so important?

*Your connection with spirit is like filling your tank up with gas. Without gas you will go nowhere. The disconnection becomes too much over an extended period of time. It is very important to recharge, to reconnect with the source, with who you are.*

So is it better actually, as I have read, to sleep twice a day and therefore dream twice a day?

*Absolutely, it would be best if you could sleep four times a day.*

Four times?

*And take intervals of long naps...instead of a long sleep. This is not always possible in your society.*

Right. Like every 5 hours sleep for an hour?

*There is one of your humans who did this and was quite successful. His name was Leonardo da Vinci. He adopted this pattern of waking and sleeping and quite wondrous things came from him.*

Four times a day?

*Indeed.*

Long naps like an hour or two?

*Yes, instead of eight or ten hours of sleep all at once.*

Right. And that's enough time to dream?

*Indeed it is. If all you take are naps you will go right into the dream state and you will remember more of your dreams, too, which would allow you to incorporate more of your dream life into your waking life, which would allow you to create those things that geniuses create because you are in effect walking the line between two realities. You have your source entity on one side, and your human life on the other, and if you sleep often they are so well incorporated that constant inspiration is coming from source energy. It is not just in the morning or just at certain intervals during the day when you might have a rush of energy. It is constant. It is all the time. Energy. Inspiration. Impetus to create. Action and the wherewithal, the energy, the inspiration to do it.*

So it would be good to be on a planet that had a faster rotation so that it had many days and nights in the same 24 hour period that we deal with.

*Perhaps that would work better. It is not necessary.*

Why do we sleep so long at night? Is it because it is dark and we see better in the daylight? Is that why we have adopted this habit?

*Indeed, it is a habit, and societies have created themselves around the coming of the sun and moon. But it is certainly now no longer necessary. One has electricity and artificial light, and even in the cave man days one had fire. It was not always necessary to be asleep at night, and sometimes it was more desirable to be awake.*

Right. So also regarding dreams, there are books on dreams about interpretation of certain symbols. Does that mean anything, or is meaning specific to the person?

*It is extremely specific to the individual. However, there are archetypal symbols, which can apply to many people. A Christ symbol, for example, is archetypal, a symbol of love and sacrifice for many, but not for everyone.*

So if somebody saw Jesus in their dreams it may only be a symbol for something that Jesus means to them.

*Yes. It is likely.*

Could it also be a visit from the dead?

*Of course it could be. Regarding a dream vision of Jesus, in your society, most often it is not a visit from the dead man. The Jesus who walked Earth would be more likely to visit those he actually knew and there are very few people who knew the actual man. However, there are a few incarnations walking Earth today who knew Jesus in a different incarnation.*

Are those people automatic Christians?

*Most often they are not Christians. The message has been too diluted, and so most of those who had incarnations with Jesus now call themselves mystics or some other form of spirituality.*

Did you know Jesus, the man?

*I have an incarnation who briefly met Jesus when he was a young man. He had heard of him, briefly met him, was pleased to meet him, and then went on with his own life. Bharfius was his name. He was a merchant.*

Okay, back to the topic of dreams. What is a common misconception that we have about dreams?

*You think that they are imaginations of the brain. You think that they are based purely on your physical life. That they have no grounding in the spiritual, when in fact they are mostly spiritual. The brain can assist, but there are places that the spirit goes that the brain cannot reach at all. There are times when the brain is dead to the world, so to speak. If your scientists hooked you up to a machine they would see no brain activity and yet you would be dreaming. So if you sleep very, very deeply you would be having experiences on planes far, far away from your consciousness as you know it now.*

So that is basically an out-of-body experience?

*Indeed.*

So, many dreams are literally out-of-body experiences?

*Yes.*

But not all dreams?

*Everyone leaves their body every night if they have a full amount of sleep.*

We just take off and go somewhere?

*Yes. There are things that you cannot do while you are in your body. There are things you can do; light dreams you can have while you are still in your physical body. However, there are many things that are impossible to do unless you leave* your physical body. You are still connected to your physical body by energy. You are energetically connected, so if someone were to try to rouse you or if something were to happen, you would awaken because of the energetic connection. However, you are not inhabiting your physicality at that juncture.

So, when we go to sleep we always take off if we can and go somewhere, and this helps us reconnect to our source energy?

*Yes, it also helps you explore and bring back fodder for your existence here. It is always a give-and-take, an exchange. Taking fodder from your existence here, you go off and play there with this raw material of ideas and experiences, and then you bring back some more fodder to play with here, you see. It is an exchange: bringing something from that energy to this one and taking something from this energy to that one.*

---

Do two people ever dream at the same time and go to the same place?

*Yes. It can happen. Two people can agree to meet, and meet at the same location at the same time.*

Do they have to consciously agree to do this?

*It is not necessary to consciously agree to do it. However this makes it more likely, and also more likely that both parties will remember the occurrence.*

So when I dream of somebody that I know and they are in my dream, are they actually in my dream with me, or is it just part of them, or just my idea of them?

*It depends on the situation. Sometimes it is them, and sometimes a part of them, or sometimes it is you being them in your dream. But it is possible for them to appear entirely as themselves in your dreams.*

So sometimes it is just my perception of them that I brought with me?

*Yes.*

## Dreams

I see, because after all, my perception of them is usually simply my view of their physical self here, and not entirely of their spiritual self.

*That is correct. But if they are trying to reach you in a dream or otherwise, they will usually appear in a form that is comfortable for you.*

---

So, do we get visits from dead people in dreams?

*Yes, it happens all the time, much more often than people might suppose. The dead are close to you, they are constantly trying to reconnect, and it is a very easy plane for them to get to. It is also an easy plane for you to get to, and so you often meet in the middle. There are many variations of different planes in the dream world. Therefore, there are many planes on which to meet, and this makes it a veritable playground for the living and the dead to meet up. Or should I say, the living and the non-living; although, perhaps even that is not quite accurate.*

Perhaps we could refer to the dead as those that have crossed over.

*Indeed. But there is no real crossing over. You are as you are. And you are always you. Everything is permanent and impermanent at the same time. This moment lasts forever, and yet the opposite is also true.[3] We will discuss this more in the chapter on the Death Experience.*

So when people visit with the dead in their dreams, is it because we have a desire to talk to them? Do people miss them, or is it the other way around? Do the non-living spirits want to talk to us?

*A connection is desired from the living. Those that are gallivanting in other realities feel this pull and they therefore desire contact. The illusion of time is very strong on your plane, and the same is true of the illusion of separation. So on the other planes*

---

[3] The reader would do well to remember that this is how we are from Brahma's perspective. It is often not so easy to think of things this way from our limited physical existence. We feel separated and we experience change in who we are and these moments can seem fleeting. The experience of crossing over is discussed more in Chapter 7, The Death Experience.

~ 41 ~

*where those who are non-living have, as you say, crossed over, there is no need for feelings of urgency, or sadness, or that feeling that you often get here that you will never see the person again. In fact, those on the other plane feel as though they will see you again in the next moment. However, they feel the pull and wish to contact you for they wish to comfort those who are left behind, so to speak, especially those who do not understand that separation is an illusion, and those who do not understand that time is an illusion. In truth, there is no separation and no time.*

So to the non-living there is not really urgency in terms of time to meet, it's more or less that they are drawn to comfort those who are needing the contact.

*That is correct. Those who feel lost are desirous of contact with those they have been close to.*

Okay, I see. Allow me to ask a few more dream questions: When I have a dream and I can actually remember what happened in the dream, how do I know what is important and what things are just insignificant musings?

*You do not know what is important to you?*

Well I think I do, but sometimes I'll have a dream that I remember when I wake up and I have no idea what it was about. I wonder why I had that dream and whether there was an important reason for it.

*There is not always a discernible important reason. Sometimes a dream is important to someone you have a spiritual connection with, or to a fragment of yourself. And it is not as important to you, but you have helped this fragment along. Sometimes, of course, it is more about you, and you are more involved. Generally speaking, when you awaken from these dreams, you will feel the significance of it and perhaps take some inspired action or have a new insight. You might wake up with it, or have some insight or inspiration later on during the day.*

So you are saying that when it becomes important I'll recognize it.

Now, sometimes when I dream about something, I wonder if it may be a sort of premonition of what I might experience, but I won't realize it until I actually have that experience.

*Coming attractions.*

Yes. Is there a way to know what is a coming attraction and what is not?

*You must focus on previewing coming attractions if that is your wish. There is no real way to know unless you make a habit of it, and focus on it. You can get good at it as you can get good at many other skills. But if you are just dabbling, say for instance, in golf you may hit a perfect ball once in a while, but you won't really know how to hit that perfect ball unless you practice. It's the same in foretelling future events. You must practice and focus on it to develop the skill by focusing and concentrating on it while having desire to do it.*

Okay, so you could practice, and if you made an effort to focus on future events with desire, then you could develop a talent for fortune telling?

*Yes, it is a skill. Though some are born with this skill, it is somewhat rare in your society for people to know for sure of a coming attraction. There are individuals who can do this. But most are not just born with it, and most do not care to put the focus of intention on it.*

Okay. So if I have a dream that turns out to be a premonition, it's probably just sort of a lucky shot, like in golf?

*Yes, precisely.*

And I shouldn't expect to be able to recognize it as a premonition when I have the dream because I haven't been practicing or focusing on it?

*That is correct, although sometimes you will get an especially strong warning, but the dream will not usually be an exact foretelling of events. It will be given to you in symbols and you will act on it because of the strong feelings you have associated with it. Do you understand this?*

Yes, so you have a strong feeling about the dream because it will pull in symbols that have a lot of meaning to you to interpret the dream.

*Yes, you may have a dream about a mouse going into a hole when the dream is actually representative of a train going into a tunnel that you will be on. You see it might not be the exact thing, not in the same way you are thinking of, it will be a symbol that will cause you to act.*

And if the dream is important to me, then I might see a mouse if mice were really important to me, and it would induce a strong feeling and then I would be prompted to act?

*Yes, and if there were, say, a mousetrap in that hole, and you dreamed that the mouse was hurt by it, perhaps something irregular would happen on the train that would cause you to get hurt. And so you are dreaming of the mouse, but later on you decide to take the train on an alternative day. You might not realize why but you might feel overwhelmed and too busy to take the trip that day. Do you understand?*

Oh, okay. So the mouse is just a metaphor that might instill in me a significant feeling. And I may or may not even recognize that the mouse was an analogy for the train. It may even be all subconscious.

*Exactly. But if you were to become skilled at recognizing coming attractions, you could just as easily have the dream about the train.*

Okay.

---

So I have read that it's good to write down my dreams. I think you recommended that everyone should try to know what they are dreaming about.

*Absolutely. Recording your dreams will help you recall them. Knowing your dreams helps to connect you with your greater self and your greater selves. You are part of one great entity that is many, and it connects you to those and helps you be less focused on this reality and more focused on your greater reality, which is good for your evolution. Now I do not mean by this that you should ignore your waking reality; it is an important focus for you. However, it is good to be reminded that you really are more than this.*

# CHAPTER 4
## YOU ARE NOT REINCARNATED

This discussion with Brahma about reincarnation clarifies the misconceptions of how reincarnation actually works with respect to each soul. We see how each new life has a freshly minted soul and there really is no recycling of souls.

*Good afternoon.*

Good afternoon, Brahma. Welcome.

*Why thank you my friend.*

We have spoken about soul-fragments and other selves, and I thought we could continue with the book and talk about reincarnation. Shall we?

*That is an excellent proposal.*

I think the whole idea of past lives needs some clarification.

*Indeed. A confusing subject for many who think they understand it.*

Yes, yes. I think the popular concept involves living, then dying, then being born again into a new body. When moving into a new body, most all memories are erased. They are erased similar to the way files are erased on the memory of a computer. They are erased but they can somehow sometimes be re-accessed even though they have been deleted.

*This is a distorted version as you may already realize.*

Yes, it seems a little inconsistent with a lot of my understanding. So I guess my first question is: Do we actually reuse our souls by reinserting them into new bodies?

*Not in a sense that most people on this planet consider to be true. Not in the sense that you would transfer water into a new container. Not in this sense. The soul is always expanding and growing bigger. Energy is always added to it. So if you think of the soul as if it were a physical object, it would be expanding in space in volume or size, you see. Atom upon atom, growing larger and larger. The soul, for a reincarnation, does not simply re-purpose the same energy that has already been incarnated as, say, a carpenter or a lawyer. The soul draws on all of its energies, including those experiences acquired by the carpenter and lawyer, and it creates a freshly minted soul. Every incarnation or reincarnation is a freshly minted soul gathered from energies that have been rejoined into the entity after what you consider to be the death experience.*

So, an entity or larger collection of souls is getting experience and growing larger in a sense, adding soul energy, like how adding material to a physical object makes it larger.

*Yes, it is like adding energy. I know you are a very visual people and if you think of it in terms of space, you might be able to conceptualize it a little better. In reality of course energy takes up no space. Yet if you collect energy you are bigger in a sense.*

Yes. So it's more like an add-on incarnation as opposed to a reincarnation?

*In a sense what you say is true; however, we can add "re-" to the beginning of this if we think of it in terms of adding experience from the carpenter or the lawyer into the new soul, if you understand what I am meaning. Is this clear?*

I think so. Perhaps the soul is "re-employed as a lawyer" except that only some of the experience energy of the carpenter is in the new soul, but not the carpenter's memories.

*The memories could actually be there. There have been children, most often in India, who have had memories of past lives. But these are memories of incarnations that are close to them, very close to them. Their souls have drawn a lot on these previous incarnations. They have taken a lot of energy from, say, the carpenter to become this new child in India. So they may have what seems like memories though they are* not *actual memories. Although, it becomes more complicated if you consider that they could be thought of as consisting of* all *of their previous incarnations because they* are *the entity in a sense. The entity is comprised of all of these incarnations. Are you understanding this?*

Yes, I think so. So it is similar to, maybe, the recycling of a plastic bottle in the respect that it is mixed with other plastic bottles and melted down. It can become a new plastic bottle or something else. It is not simply reused.

*It is not the same plastic bottle.*

Right.

*It is energy created anew, sort of like giving birth to a new soul. It is an entity that is becoming more of itself by giving birth to new energy. It is like creating a piece of art. There was nothing but paint and canvas before, but now there is art. There is still paint and canvas but the artwork is new. Or if you prefer, if you were to have a child. Although you, Robert, are not a creator of people, many other people can relate to this. It would be like that. There was nothing and now there is a child. And the child is new, not recycled, but is from the biological material of the parents.*

Right. The child comes from the parents and it could retain some physical aspects of the parents?

*The child does in the form of DNA. The child retains eye color, physique, skin color, even mental characteristics, and things like this on the physical plane.*

Yes.

*With a new soul, there are often similarities, but not always.*

So it works the same way in that with a new soul they are retaining some of the characteristics of their "parents" or the larger entity from which they came. Experience energy is passed on in a similar way that a genetic legacy is passed on.

*Yes, and do you understand that if the entire entity is considered to be a collection of souls, this newly minted soul would be another soul added to the collection? So the entity would become larger every time it chooses to incarnate. It is an expansive energy, a new energy, a freshly minted energy like a new child in the world.*

So, with the expansion of energy, is there an evolution of souls? Are people born today better off than those born long ago at an earlier time?

*There is no time to a soul.[4] So in this light you will need to clarify your question.*

If an entity becomes larger in experience each time a new one is created, it would seem to me that a child born today would have the benefit of the experience of many historical incarnations.

*Yes, if that is your question, the answer is yes. More experience appears to be beneficial and the soul ever craves evolution and new creation. This it considers to be progress. So yes, a new incarnation or child born of an entity that has had many experiences and is a larger collection will have much more experience to draw upon and to step off of in terms of its own soul evolution.*

But that's not to say that all new born children have a large number of souls behind them?

*Not necessarily. It is individual depending on the entity of course. And not all entities incarnate on your plane. Some incarnate on their own planes and some never incarnate. Some do not have the ability and some do not have the desire for your earthly experience. It is a specialized plane that you live on and, I might add, one that is much unappreciated by its inhabitants.*

Okay, so it doesn't work exactly the way that a lot of people think it does. It's not like buying new cars. You're not just putting your soul back into a new body each time. Correct?

*That is correct. One could think of it this way but only because it is the souls who are part of the same larger entity. However, to me it seems to not be the same as each soul is freshly minted and new. It is not just a new physical creation. It is a new soul. Each new carpenter makes its own memories. These memories, as we just spoke of, are not typically passed on to the new child. The new child creates its own memories.*

But are they affected by the carpenter in some ways?

*Yes, and the carpenter is affected by the new child as well. Yes, it is a give and take of energy. The child can draw upon the skill of the carpenter but the child is separate from the carpenter yet of the same the energy. This is complicated. So they*

---

[4] **Brahma resides in a reality outside of our convention of time. He tends to see souls in the same light as living outside of time.**

*are separate, yet could be considered to be the same. Perhaps I can clarify by drawing on our former tree analogy. The child is a leaf but not the branch. It is another leaf of the tree, separate but of the same tree. The new leaf is fresh in this world; the tree is old. The leaf gets nutrients from the tree and the tree benefits from the leaf.*

Okay. So how does reincarnation affect the new soul? People have reported that they are afraid of something for no known reason, and they attribute that to an event in a previous life. They say it's because of something traumatic that has happened in another life.

*Sometimes the energy of the newly minted soul is affected by an energy that is part of its greater entity that is close in terms of, shall we say, vibration or energy frequency. Perhaps the soul has come from an idea generated by the carpenter who drowned, let's say. So the new soul energy will have a similar vibration to that of the carpenter and it will have characteristics based on the source of the energy. The new soul arises into the world to do its own thing, but because it inherited energy from the carpenter it is afraid of water because the carpenter had drowned. This does not mean this new soul had ever actually experienced drowning. But a part of its greater entity did. A part that is close to it. Or it may not be from the carpenter at all. It can be from a soul energy that is similar in vibration, similar in quality or energetically close which affects this newly minted soul.*

Okay.

*If anything does not make sense, please help us clarify.*

I think it does. So are there memories that somebody can access from a previous life? Is that something that is directly related to the reincarnation thing or is that just somebody being able to access information from brother entities?

*Well it is not brother entities, it is the same entity. All of the reincarnations come from the same entity and that is why it is a reincarnation. If you are incarnated and Bronwen is incarnated this is not a reincarnation because you are separate entities. You have your own incarnations and I have mine. If this is understood.*

So, Bronwen is a kind of reincarnation of Brahma?

*Yes.*

As are other soul-fragments you have mentioned, like Zillaphia or Bharfius?

*Yes, this is correct. You are not a reincarnation of this same entity. You have your own entity.*

But Zillaphia and Bronwen are not reincarnations of each other. Are they reincarnations of Brahma?

*Yes, that is correct, though Bronwen does have a little bit of Zillaphia in her. In creating Bronwen I used a little bit of the experience of Zillaphia. She was feminine in a way that I used to help create the femininity of Bronwen. This entity was in need of more feminine energy so this was important, and this entity needed it to draw on its own energies to create this. Zillaphia was a success in this way and therefore, to expand this energy, we created Bronwen.*

Okay, that makes sense.

*Good.*

Now, when a freshly minted soul is created, that is something that is created by you, Brahma, for example. Can it be created by other parts or soul-fragments of your entity?

*It can be created by any of my soul-fragments as well as by me. Although, I tend to do more of the conscious creating of these soul-fragments.*

Okay. So, in that respect you are more of a creator of souls?

*I am more experienced at it.*

So, in a way, you are a more experienced god?

*Yes. I have had more time, so to speak. Although this expression is tricky since time is of absolutely no use to us.*

So if Bronwen can create new souls, is this something that she would do after she dies?

*She can do this consciously after she dies. She does this by accident at times and she does it consciously in the dream state as well, though these are the deeper dreams that you often cannot bring through. You do not remember these as well as other dreams, generally speaking.*

Okay. I was just wondering if I have the power to create new souls and if I do, how is that going to benefit me when I seem to be so focused on this physical body?

*If you are curious about being a virtuoso musician, you can create one. If you do not have the time to do it in this life, you can let a soul-fragment do it for you so you do not miss out on the experience.*

Okay. But I won't necessarily know this new soul-fragment?

*No, you will not necessarily. However, you will be getting satisfying feedback from this fragment and you may experience this fragment in your dreaming states.*

Right. That makes more sense. I guess I'm trying to clarify the idea that this smaller part of my entity, this soul-fragment that I call Robert is not just this physical body. Most of us here feel very individual, very separate. Most of the time, we feel like this physical existence is all there is to life. A lot of us feel like there is probably more to it, but we don't really seem to have access to that larger part of us all the time, especially to the power that we actually have.

*Yes, you do not feel you do. You do not focus on it or concentrate on it. Conscious creation would be possible, but you do not realize it or focus on it, and so during your waking hours most of your soul-fragment creations happen by accident. This does not discount the fragment in any way. Just because it was created by accident does not make it a lesser fragment.*

So conscious creation of new soul-fragments is possible.

*Indeed.*

We just may not be conscious of the new soul-fragment afterwards.

*Only the way you usually connect with other soul-fragments, such as in the dream state.*

---

Okay. What about people who have reported that they have done past-life regressions where they remember back to their birth and they are able to remember further back to a previous life? What does this mean and how does this work?

*You are connecting with the soul energy and remembering incarnations of your entire entity. Just because it was not exactly you going through these past life experiences, it does not mean that it is not valid. They are experiences of the larger soul. They are incarnations of the entity and therefore they are* you. *Just as Brahma has created Bronwen, so Bronwen is Brahma yet she is* not. *I am my own entity and she is hers, however we are energetically connected because she came from me. And if she can remember experiences from Zillaphia or Bharfius she is in a sense remembering her own experiences because those experiences are hers to draw on, and she was created from some of the energy of those experiences.*

Okay. A friend of mine mentioned that when he did a past life regression he felt as if it was just him in different clothes. Does this have a lot to do with his own self-concept? Would that imply he is just more in touch with his larger entity?

*It would, and also this friend's entity has a lot of successful repetition. There are characteristics about this friend that seem to be successful. The entity likes to replicate many of these successful qualities because this friend has had rapid growth and so like a successful product it continues to be repeated. There are many others of his entity that are like him. So this can seem as though it is him and of course, in a way, it is.*

So it just seems to be very much like himself? Much more so than it would if he connected to part of his entity trying some new aspect with a soul-fragment?

*Yes because this friend, this friend's entity has a tendency to recreate itself in terms of the successful parts of it. And it has many successful parts. So it is like a chef adjusting a very good recipe, you see. "It is working well but let's see if we can do it a slightly different way."*

Okay. Very good.

*However, keep in mind that your friend's experiences are valid. He is seeing it in a different way than I am describing it from my perspective.*

Some religions believe that there is a reincarnation scale where you are reincarnated as an animal and work your way up to human. Can we be reincarnated from animals to humans? Or even from humans to animals?

*As I have explained you are not reincarnations of anything. However, if you wish, you can have animals or humans or a collection of different incarnations in your entity. It is based on the nature of the entity. Some entities are exclusively humans or exclusively animals. Some are multidimensional and incarnate as many things and in many forms, some of which you can barely imagine. It is not a progression as some earthly religions seem to take it. You could see it that way. But it is not as though you become a beast because you act like one, or become a pig because you act like a glutton. It is not like this. However, if you were a glutton and you wanted to experience your gluttony to the fullest, and you thought that being a pig would be a fine way to do it, you might create one that was not you but of you to experience the energy, to experience the fullness of gluttony which some might decide is a waste of time. However, nothing is a waste of time to the soul, and experiencing the fullness of something like gluttony can be satisfying to the soul from an evolutionary point of view. You cannot truly know something unless you have experienced it, even if it seems undesirable.*

Right. So an entity might choose to incarnate or create different types of people or different types of animals just for the experience of it?

*Yes, it is all just for the experience. It is for the experience and the evolution of the soul.*

But it's never directly, like in a linear progression.

*It is never linear. Except in your timeframe it appears to be. But this is a construct of the human mind and the body consciousness or ego. This is not the reality of things.*

So by that token it cannot apply to something that is not living at times. Somebody lives and then dies. Their life is experienced in a linear way, but after that you can't draw lines to other lives.

*Even their lives are not linear in the way that you think of it. It will seem so to you and it seems quite impossible usually to think of it any other way. But even your lives are not linear, they just appear to be.*

So, when a new child is created or incarnated they have the energy characteristics that the larger entity chooses to incorporate into that child.

*Yes, and most often they are inspired by an experience that the entity has had and a new idea stemming from that experience.*

So they may be born with certain characteristics and maybe even certain talents. Could they have any memories or knowledge?

*They could, depending on what the entity chooses to give them or what they choose to accept into their own incarnation. They may have that if they choose it and if the entity chooses it for them or they may not.*

So is that something that they could optionally choose after they have been born?

*One can try to access these things and acquire them that way.*

So you could try being a painter and realize you have some sort of propensity for that.

*Absolutely, there are many incarnates walking around with untapped talents that they could access if they chose, if they were interested.*

So it's not as if they knew something and then they have forgotten it in order to become this person, it is just that they were created with certain characteristics or energies and they are free to recall, or rather call up, things or the experiences of other aspects of their larger entity.

*Yes, they are. There may be energies that are so far removed from them that they would be in a sense blocked, but for the most part, yes. They can be called upon, these experiences of the entity from which it sprang. And there is of course, the whole idea of forgetting. And it is a forgetting, however, it is also a not-knowing. You are almost in a sense cast adrift as a freshly minted soul, and so you might not understand the way of the world or even where you came from. When you "came from your parents" you only knew this because they told you, otherwise you would not really understand it. And so as you progress along your newly minted life you are evolving and starting to understand these things.*

That makes a lot more sense.

*I am pleased. Explaining this is not as easy as it looks.*

No, and people talk about reincarnation as if everybody understands the idea. Often, people either believe in reincarnation or they don't. But it never made sense to me the way people always described it. I just thought their definition wasn't accurate.

*You are correct. You have good, as they say in this reality, horse sense? Although there are very few horses with this sense.*

Yes, that may be true.

---

Now, I know there are some religions that don't believe in reincarnation simply because of the fact that there are far more people today than there used to be.

*But of course, this makes perfect sense does it not?*

But this idea also seems to be sort of a logical answer that lacks any depth of knowledge. Because by their logic, there could have always been a bank of souls on hand where they could just be dispensed any time the overall population grew.

*Indeed. And this is not the case.*

No.

*The souls are newly minted, always.*

So souls are not reused but they are conserved, especially in the respect that they are not thrown away, eliminated.

*No, certainly not. An entity retains all of its souls. It is a little collection. It is a little collection that expands and expands and becomes bigger and they all stick together because they are an energetic source of intelligence. And they just get bigger. And of course if the entity is so inclined, it can cast off two or three or five freshly minted incarnates at the same time into different realities, into different zones, different levels of your Earth, different times. They can all be continuing and freshly minted at once. The entity could say, "Aha, I've got it! Let me make this one, and this one, and I'll make this one just for good measure as a combination of the two just to make sure I get the experience."*

So they can exist in different times. Could they exist at the same time? Would that be too complicated?

*They can. It doesn't happen very often because it is too close of an experience, unless there is a significant geographical separation. Some entities will do this but if they have the idea of what they want they will cast it where they want it. If they want something slightly different, usually they will put it somewhere else.*

So there's no advantage to them being at the same time and place if they were going for a specific experience.

*Well, I suppose they could meet up. There is no rule against it, but again, this is not a usual practice. If they could meet up perhaps they could help each other, but then of course they would be so energetically similar that they might have nothing at all to say to each other.*

Right.

*They might acknowledge their relationship on a spiritual level and then move on.*

Right, there might not be much benefit to the interaction.

*It is not the usual. That is not to say it cannot or has not happened. It is just not customary and not for reasons of "this is how it is done" or anything of this sort, but just for reasons of practicality.*

Okay, that makes a lot more sense.

*We are relieved. It is difficult to explain these things in terms of your language and linear thought patterns at times.*[5]

---

[5] It would seem that the perception of time by Brahma who exists without time is clouding our understanding of the idea of two personalities of the same entity existing at the same time. The word coinciding might be a better term than at the same time. Considering that in our physical existence, time is always space-time and to someone observing from outside our time and reality, the phrase *at the same time* may be confused with *at the same place*.

It is. And I think it is compounded by a lot of misconceptions that are running about in our knowledge circles here.

*Indeed, and there are probably many people who would not be too happy to hear this. That it is quite different than the way they are thinking of it. On the other hand, some people may feel freed by the information.*

Right. Much like our last discussion, it might also be information some might not like to hear just like the idea that their definition of God is not what they think it is.

*Indeed. People are very protective of their definitions of God and they must go with whatever is going to provide the most evolution for them.*

I agree. Everyone must progress at their own pace.

---

That is all the questions I have regarding reincarnation. You have helped clarify a lot for me.

*Good. We are pleased that we have explained ourselves well and thank you for the excellent questions. You have led us in a most excellent direction and have enabled us to explain many things we wish to convey. It has been a most pleasant evening. We appreciate the chance to express ourselves and share with you our information. Thank you very much, Robert.*

Thank you very much, Brahma. I appreciate it, too. It is always a pleasure.

*Indeed.*

Good night then.

# CHAPTER 5
## THE LIFE EXPERIENCE

In this chapter, our conversation touches on the idea that all matter and life has consciousness and our reality is created with agreements on the part of all consciousness. There are spiritual agreements that influence our lives but our destiny is changeable. Brahma also explains the nature of love and its role in our experience. We finish with an interesting and somewhat complicated explanation of the nature of time as seen from Brahma's perspective, who operates largely outside of our space and time.

*Good evening.*

Good evening, Brahma. Welcome.

*It is a pleasure.*

It's my pleasure as well.

*We are adjusting to the connection, as usual.*

Thank you for the session last time. I think we got a lot of very good information.

*You had many astute questions. It was appreciated. We were able to convey some knowledge that is not always asked about but is important, nonetheless.*

Thank you. It's nice to have someone to ask.

*It is my pleasure, as always.*

Our next chapter is entitled The Life Experience. It seems like quite a general topic. Honestly, I'm not really sure what it is you might want talk about.

*It is more specifically referring to the life experience of an incarnation on your planet.*

Okay. So as opposed to another planet or another type of incarnation?

*Or an alternate reality, of which there are many.*

Okay. So, specifically it relates to my life and Bronwen's life and likely that of the reader?

*That is correct, and the energies of those with which you share your reality.*

Okay. Well, that leads me to a question. Some people have theorized that our reality and our perception of it exists only in our individual minds. Do we actually share this reality? Does it exist independently from our perception?

*Yes, it is created with the energy of all who share it. And by all, I mean every energy of this planet, including energies that you do not consider to be alive, like for instance, rocks. You would not ordinarily think of them as having a contributing consciousness. However, they do. They all contribute to the creation of your reality.*

So it's not just biological life. It's Earth and everything it encompasses. Does all matter have sort of a consciousness? I've read that all matter has an energy equivalence. Is consciousness a form of energy?

*Yes. That is correct.*

So, if consciousness is a form of energy, and all matter has consciousness, then all matter has energy. Which is what we would expect, as Einstein postulated. You are saying that part of this energy in all matter is made up of consciousness and every bit of matter here on Earth plays a role in the creation of this reality?

*Yes, every consciousness contributes to the energy of its reality. It contributes to the many different experiences in its reality. The experience of two different lives can vary in great degrees within the same reality.*

So, shall we call this reality the Earth experience?

*If it pleases you.*

It does. Because that seems to encompass the life of humans, the life of rocks, trees and everything on Earth.

*Yes, although most humans reading this material would probably be a bit more interested in the human aspects of it, I imagine.*

Of course. There may not be many people who spend a lot of time wondering what it's like to be a rock.

*But a few of you do.*

Of that I am sure. So, I have another question: How is this life a co-creation of the contributing energies, and in what ways is it a solo creation?

*That is indeed a complex question.*

Sorry.

*Nonetheless, we will do our best. All energies that participate in this reality contribute to its form and its basic character—you have of course certain laws of physics. You have general agreements about certain types of things such as: the sun shall rise in the east and it shall set in the west. There are trees that exchange carbon dioxide for oxygen. Humans need oxygen to breathe without which they cannot survive. In water, one can float or one can sink depending upon the circumstances. These things are all agreed upon collectively by all of life and consciousness. Time is agreed upon also by all of you. These things that are agreements can change. They sometimes do from century to century.*

*It takes a long time in your Earth years to facilitate changes with this kind of thing. For instance, Earth for all practical intents and purposes, used to be flat. It was a different universe back then. Now you all laugh and say, "How foolish they were." But Earth was more flat than round at that point. When someone has an idea about something and it spreads into the collective consciousness, it can change the properties of where you live. It can change time. It can change physics. These are co-created aspects of your reality.*

*Now, your solo creation is that which you choose to experience of this life within the accepted agreements and laws of physics created by all of you. You do not have to live in a war-torn area. You do not have to be a prince and live in a palace. However both of these options are available to you. You may focus on making a grand change in the world or you may focus on creating a single piece of art privately in your lifetime. You may focus on human relationships or relationships with the animals or with Earth. The solo creation is affected by your focus.*

So, basically directing where we focus our energy is the best way of controlling our solo experience?

*Yes, the solo experience is devised by focus, and solo experience varies greatly within this collective experience.*

Because, I often wonder about the specific events in my life. Sometimes I think, "Oh, that situation has something to do with what I have focused on." Other times it seems that it has something to do with what has happened to me, as if it were a contribution of other energies involved besides me. So, that's why I ask how much of it is solo and how much of it is sort of a co-creation of contributing efforts or energies with other parts of the energy of the Earth experience. I wonder how much of every event in my life is of my own device.

*The energies are moving back and forth all of the time. Sometimes 70% of your experience is solo. Sometimes it is 50%. It is depending upon how swayed you are by other energies and outside influences, and this varies within your lifetime as it varies moment to moment. Things can happen in the collective which you can choose to accept or reject in your personal experience. You can be part of a flood or you can refuse to participate by being absent, you see.*

Yes. But nevertheless the flood happens because that is a collective co-creation.

*It is agreed upon by those energies in the area of the flood and by Earth and collective consciousness as a whole. But it does not have to affect you personally unless you agree to be personally affected by it.*

Now, how much of this personal agreement, or even the amount that we focus on something, is up to me, the conscious Robert, and how much of it is affected by the larger me, the contribution of my entire entity?

*Again, this is very individual. The entity sets you forth for a specific reason in order to gain a specific experience or obtain a specific balance. You are given free will but once you are set on a path it is not easy to do an about face. If you have come here to have the experience of poverty and you decide you would rather be rich, it is against your nature because the entity sent you forth for the different purpose. This does not mean you cannot be rich, but it is difficult for your consciousness to change so abruptly. It is, shall we say, your program but not your hardware. You see, you were created with the program, though it can be rewritten and changed.*

So it's not my destiny.

*No. It is a likelihood and it is important to the larger entity. And working in harmony with the entity, you would do your best to fulfill its needs. Its needs are your needs also.*

So maybe the destiny is just the path that one is on, where they are going. The direction they are heading can be changed, but that is the direction they are already facing.

*Yes.*

So when something unfortunate happens to someone, they might say, "Hey, I didn't agree to this." But it's likely that they actually did in some way?

*This can occur. If you spend your time thinking a lot about floods and you really, really don't want to be in a flood, your entity and the consciousness of the world hears 'flood' and 'you'. And you will unwittingly draw yourself to this. You do not feel it is an agreement, but it is, you see. You have put emotional energy into it. Therefore it is a form of agreement.*

When I have focused on it, I have agreed to it?

*Yes. It is not a typical agreement in terms of the way you think of things. But the universe, of which you are a part, the collective consciousness of the universe that we are calling Earth in this case, hears that you are attracted to a flood. Whether it is positive or negative coming from your small consciousness is immaterial to the larger consciousness of the world.*

Okay. That is a very good answer and a very interesting scenario.

*I am glad if you find it helpful.*

Being that this is a reality created by many different energies here on Earth, I'm curious about the effects that I have on others and the effects of others on me. I guess, specifically, if we have agreements on things like laws of physics and time and floods, are there also agreements between others and me on encounters and meetings and things that people do for each other that significantly affect parts of other people's lives?

*Yes, there are things that are agreed to before you incarnate, meetings that are supposed to happen, energies that are supposed to help you in the form of people or animals or even things that you would consider to be made up of inanimate earth.*

*These agreements can be broken but they are not often broken. There are also chance meetings. When energy is attracted to like energy, things just happen. But yes, there is a structure to a life experience in a sense that there are some planned meetings.*

But there probably isn't much of a way to know how much planning has gone into, say, an encounter between two people because it may change? I understand that if I decide to go visit somebody that I've made a conscious decision to do that. But I am more questioning when it seems like I've been thrown into the area with somebody else, seemingly thrown into a situation. How much of that is chance? How much of that is like energies being attracted and how much of it was an agreed upon decision?

*Often, you will know when you come across agreed upon individuals, if you are in touch with your intuition.*

So, one's intuition can be an indicator of a spiritual agreement?

*Yes. There are children who have agreed to be born to certain sets of parents. There are husbands and wives or brothers and sisters who have agreed to meet. There are friends who have agreed to meet at certain points along the lifeline to assist each other. There is usually a very good connection with those whom you have agreed to meet. Sometimes meetings are put off because energies have not evolved as expected. If your entity sets you down on a certain path and you have gone the other way, the personality or energy who has agreed to meet you may not be so much help now and may or may not come to the meeting, as it were.*

So it can change? Agreements can change?

*Yes. It is only kept if it is beneficial.*

---

I have another question regarding the life experience. I can't help but ask it. Is there a higher meaning to life? If so, what is the meaning of life?

*It is to gain experience. I have said before that the entity is hungry for experience, experience of all kinds. And with every experience comes a need for the entirety of the experience and therefore a need for balance. So, life is a constant searching for experience and then a searching for balance. Experience then balance, then experience, then balance. An incarnation, or life as you are referring to it, is an opportunity for knowledge. The entity thirsts for knowledge and for experience. Direct experience provides the most intimate knowledge.*

So that is the meaning of life? That is the purpose of life?

*That is the purpose: experience and knowledge. All types of experience. Even the experience of boredom is important to the entity. If you spend a life bored it is not necessarily wasted.*

Because it has value as an experience?

*Yes. You have after all an eternity to gain this experience.*

How does love fit into all of this?

*Love is the force that propels the universe.*

So does that mean that love is the desire for experience?

*There is desire for experience in love. But love is more than that. Love is the center of creation. It is well-being and compassion and desire for the best for all, knowing that the best is happening for all.*

So considering that love is the force that propels the universe, can we consider it to be the energy, perhaps, behind experience? Maybe it's the part that facilitates experience itself: the living of life, the coordination of energies, or the force that every energy can use in co-creating reality.

*Yes, it is the life force but it is not just a force. It is what you would call a force for good. It is a benevolent energy. It never wishes harm. Harm may appear to come but this is not ever the wish of the entity.*

So love is always beneficial.

*It can behoove you very much to tap into love as often as you can. Love is the main line to your entity. It infuses you with the energy that is most creative. If you are speaking of emotions, although we do not call love exclusively an emotion, beneath any of your emotions is love. Beneath hatred, beneath anger, beneath the fear, beneath all of this, if you uncover them, at their source they are love. But love is so convoluted with these other emotions that it is sometimes difficult to see and difficult to get to. But if you can get to the love underneath, your creativity will be* heightened. Your experience will be more beautiful, brighter, and perhaps more interesting.

So is that what I've heard referred to as the source energy?

*Source energy is love.*

And it is the basis for all emotions?

*Yes. It is misread at times.*

Right. This love seems like a difficult thing to completely understand.

*It is a difficult thing to explain in your terms. We have words that describe it but they cannot completely tell you what it is. Words describe properties of love but in your existence you need to feel it to get a glimpse of it.*

Not quite the same as explaining a table, for instance?

*Not quite the same.*

So, love is the force that propels the universe, and is also the source energy with which we can connect to give us creative energy?

*Yes. Love is the energy that fuels all of the entities, all of the energy in the universe. Connecting to your particular source is connecting to an energy that is connected to this love. So it is similar you see, because it is all an energy. But you are connecting to your particular source. You can try to connect to a source beyond your original source because as you know, up and up it goes through the spiritual family tree. However, if you are looking for this love from your source energy, it is easiest for you to connect to that from which you immediately came, and so that is why you look to connect to your source. Now, it is possible to leapfrog ahead of your source and connect to energy further up. But it is not as easy, generally speaking.*

Is that energy any different?

*It is a finer type of energy the further up the tree you go, or the further back if you are thinking of it in terms of spiritual ancestry.*

Okay. When you say finer do you mean more pure?

*Yes, that will suffice for an explanation. It is more undiluted and is perhaps less able to understand you as it is a step further away. The further you go back into your energy ancestry, the less it is likely to understand your immediate problems and concerns, though it will still love you, of course.*

Okay.

*But it may not really give much care about whether you get that bill paid or not. Your immediate source may have a little more compassion for your immediate concerns.*

Okay. Now, you mentioned that beneath all of our emotions is love.

*Yes.*

And love is the basis for all emotions.

*It is love or it is fear for the lack of love. But it all has to do with love.*

So, is that why when emotions are high, there can be the whole scale of emotions, but a lot of times they're very passionately infused with energy? And that energy is derived from love?

*Yes.*

Which is why it is kind of synonymous with source energy?

*Yes. Love is the dominant energy from which all emotions spring. It is love or fear for the lack of it.*

So, is that why people can summon energy for fighting?

*They are afraid they are not loved if they are fighting, or they are not feeling love and this is why they fight. But it is all centered on love.*

Okay. So the fear of not being loved, or the fear of lack of love is all based around love. So is that why we focus on happy loving relationships, yet we also seem to be occupied with tragedies and misfortunes and injustice because we're motivated somehow by love as well as the lack thereof?

*Yes. It propels every care. In tragedy you are looking for love and it is important to find the love in tragedy which is why so many turn their heads towards it. They are looking for love within it. They are perhaps momentarily shocked that such a thing could occur with seemingly a lack of love. And so they infuse their own love into it in the form of pity perhaps or care or compassion. And they look for the love that is there.*

Okay. That sheds more light on it for me.

My next question is about the way that life experience changes from birth and being very young and then growing and being mature. The different stages of a life seem to be quite different as an experience.

*Yes.*

Is there an evolution of the soul-fragment that happens with the life experience? A growth?

*Yes, there is an evolution of the soul: There are many stages through which a life must go if it is to be a complete and long one. But there is still a teenager self of yours alive and well and experiencing. You are experiencing a different aspect of your lifeline right now. The younger you does not disappear, but continues as a younger you. You have chosen to focus on the you that is nearer to middle age at this time. You will one day focus on an older you. But the middle aged you will still exist. It is a matter of focus. Yes, there is an evolution as well, and you focus on various stages of your personality evolution in this lifetime.*

Okay. Wait, I'm confused. You say the teenage self continues?

*Yes.*

As a teenager forever?

*In a sense.*

Does it continue to have experiences?

*Yes, and it can multiply into many different experiences. It is similar to a probable self[6] in that it can go in many different directions.*

Perhaps, because it could have made or can make many different decisions?

---

[6] Probable selves and probabilities are explained more in the next chapter.

*Yes, the decisions continue even though you feel you have passed them. You can, if you wish, reach out to your teenage self and attempt to offer advice or comfort if you feel it is necessary or if a particular part of your adolescence bothers you now. It can help that teenager if you do and if the teenage self is open to it. But if you are reaching, it is a part of you so it will likely be more receptive in that case.*

So, for example if I have an unsettling experience from my teenage years, I may have feelings that are unsettling every time I think about this experience. If I am able to reach back and offer some guidance for that teenage self that is me, could that help the teenage me and therefore make the experience less traumatic?

*Yes.*

Which could then reciprocate back to me and help me as an adult?

*Yes, that is correct.*

So, by reaching to a past self or recalling an event I can help my present self come to terms with it.

*That is exactly right, and you can help other probable teenage selves as well. It is a ripple effect which could then perhaps help a childhood self or an older self.*

So, in a way it seems there is no limit to the lessons I can learn by simply reflecting upon the events of my life.

*Reflecting is one thing, offering advice and comfort or trying to change something is another thing.*

So that is the manner in which I can reach out?

*Yes.*

So, offering advice to the younger me.

*Yes, loving advice and comfort are the most helpful.*

So how would I go about that? I'm guessing I would think about my younger self and then talk to myself?

*There are a couple of different ways to do this, you can reflect on the event and speak to your younger self directly, or you can put yourself as you are now in your younger self's shoes in a situation in your mind. And you can, as you do with the animals, place thoughts in their heads.[7] You can put yourself there and act as you would now, and think as you believe would be most helpful in this situation. You can relive a situation in your mind as well, and change things that you do or that you think.*

So the idea would be to figuratively put myself in their shoes?

*Yes.*

By thinking about them and trying to understand what their experience is at that time?

*If you just understand it you will not necessarily change it, if that is your goal. You would need to change something in order to change the experience or to help, or, as you suggested, you can just talk to this self if you like.*

Okay. Is it just as effective to just talk to this self?

*It is individual. Whatever gives you the greatest sense of accomplishment and comfort. It can be beneficial to try several different methods to find the most effective one.*

Okay, I have another question: Given that I can advise a past self, it seems logical that when faced with a situation now in my present focus, I could then also ask a future, wiser me to give me some advice. Is that true?

*Ah, yes. You have discovered quite on your own a very useful technique. You absolutely can contact your future self and ask for advice. If I were you, I would be careful to select a future self who you believe is wise and successful.*

Because there are many possible future selves, some not so wise?

*That is correct and you will choose one to experience.*

But be careful which one I choose, because some might not be that bright.

*Now, they could all be models of wisdom but this is not always the case.*

---

[7] Brahma is referring to the advice he gave in a previous session where Robert asked how he could communicate with animals. The advice was roughly imagining what it is like to be that animal and having their experience, and then offering a thought that therefore becomes a suggestion to the animal.

I guess it's actually possible that some of my possible future selves could be screw ups. But nevertheless if one decides to offer me some advice, I can still accept or reject that advice. Correct?

*Absolutely, free will is always applicable.*

So, is this similar to the way a medical student who sees themselves becoming a doctor in future is therefore motivated to study difficult and maybe not so interesting concepts?

*Yes, and although it hasn't yet happened like a past experience, being a doctor in the future still contributes to the present experience.*

The more I think about this, the more my idea of a linear timeline of my life gets corrupted.

*And your idea of time should be corrupted because it has nothing to do with reality. You are all stuck in this idea of a timeline that is so extremely limiting. It is enough to make some of us watching you shake our heads, in a loving way, of course. It is not always the best thing for you. We understand that you must do this to some extent. But you might find yourself more successful if you loosen your ideas just a bit to include true reality.*

So are you saying we should think of time in ways that it is practical and helpful but always be open to the understanding that it has limited usefulness?

*Yes, that is fair to say.*

Like understanding that that chair is a solid piece of wood, but at the same time understanding that it is a conglomeration of molecules and it is basically energy and empty space.

*Yes. And as time goes on, your idea of the chair will deteriorate and so will the chair. Nevertheless, it will still be molecules and empty space, as you say.*

But for practical considerations it is handy to think of it as a solid.

*Yes. Yes, you do need some tools to navigate in the world. But thinking of past present and future in a line is not always 100% helpful since you cannot experience the past or the future the way you think of it. You have only now, you see, and you think a lot about the past and the future but you have no way of reaching it in your current frame of mind. You have no way of experiencing it unless you stretch your mind and your idea of time.*

Right, but my direct experience is always limited to my focus of the now, the present.

*That is correct.*

I can think about the future and the past.

*But if you stretch your idea of time you can experience it more fully because it is happening now as are all things. The present is eternal.*

(Once again, I am reminded that this is all so simple to Brahma who resides in a land outside of our time and is seeing things not just at our time through our eyes. With respect to all our experiences that we have from birth to death, to him it is all "happening now". I think he sees our definition of 'now' as narrow and limiting).

Right. Okay. I think I now know enough to be thoroughly confused.

*That was not our wish.*

No, I'm kidding. I understand that there is a lot to understand.

*Yes, perhaps you put your foot a bit too deep in the water?*

Maybe. But that's good. I believe that will make me a stronger swimmer.

---

I have a question that has to do with time. Time is a big deal to us, as you know, but it seems to be irrelevant to you.

*Yes, because I operate outside of it whereas you operate within it, seemingly. Your experience is focused in a reality where time is prevalent.*

Right. Does that have anything to do with the fact that you operate largely outside of our physical space as well?

*Yes, we operate outside of time and space, whereas you choose to create this artificial thing called time, and this artificial space within which to build your worlds, and to have a singular experience.*

Now, I have read that space and time are connected.

*Yes.*

We cannot move through one without moving through the other.

*Generally this is correct.*

There is always a space-time. But really it is all just the way we look at it. It is this way due to our perspective.

*What is the question?*

I guess space and time are both just something that we perceive because of our focus. There is an illusion of space, I imagine, because we think of solid objects, but we know that they are really just tiny specks of matter and energy, and they are mostly empty space.

*Yes.*

But for practical purposes they are solid.

*For your purposes.*

Yes. Can time be thought of the same way? If something we consider to be solid is mostly empty space and energy, then time is just a convention for measuring movement through that space which is not solid either.

*No, it is not solid.*

But it is really hard for us to understand that because we can't walk through walls.

*No, your beliefs forbid such a thing.*

Well, doesn't our physical body forbid that?

*Your beliefs about your physical body and your agreements in this realm forbid it.*

Okay. I understand that I could walk through a wall if I was outside of my physical body.

*Yes, of course.*

But my body is made up of the same stuff that walls are made up of, more or less.

*Yes, and so in theory if you believe you could walk through the wall, you should be able to do it. However, none of you believe this.*

But wouldn't that require an agreement of all of the consciousness of my body to get on board with that? And then wouldn't I need the consciousness of the wall to believe that as well?

*Everything would have to be agreed upon.*

Everything? Including the consciousness of the wall.

*Yes, although the wall does not care as much as you do. The wall is more open to change.*

Okay. It's good to know that walls can be agreeable.

*The wall is constructed by you. It is your belief and your perception that creates the wall. The wall does not have as much of a consciousness of its own as you do because it is you that gives it a consciousness, you see. It is your construct as a spiritual creation in addition to a physical construction.*

So what about time? Can that be separated from space? Obviously, my perception of the passage of time changes. You know, "time flies when you're having fun". But largely, when I'm measuring time, it is like, how long does it take me to get from point A to point B.

*Yes.*

Is it possible to separate the time from the space and move from point A to point B in less time?

*Well, you are already doing this with your modern airplanes.*

Well, yeah but it's also physically moving an object from one place to another place and we can do this at different rates of time. But I am wondering, if I were to travel at 100 miles per hour from point A to point B, can I make it so that it takes less time by adjusting the time or is it always going to take the same amount of time if I'm going the same speed?

*If you develop faster means to get there, say a rocket instead of an airplane, then you will effectively be changing space-time.*

But I'm still traveling at 100 miles per hour. Is there a way to stretch out the amount of time I have to get from point A to point B?

*If you take a horse, you will be stretching out the time.*

But not if the horse is running 100 miles per hour?

*The horse does not run 100 miles per hour, the horse runs 50 miles per hour. The rocket runs 1000 miles per hour. The airplane runs 500 miles per hour.*

But the physical object, the horse or the plane, cannot move outside of space and time? Like, it cannot get there before it started?

*You wish to get somewhere before you begin the journey?*

Right, time travel.

*You are asking us if time travel is possible?*

Yes, because that would be the ability to separate space and time.

*It is not possible in this immediate realm that you have situated yourself in at this moment. However, in realms similar to yours it is possible and it is also possible to cross over into these realms.*

You mean just spiritually or physically?

*They are the same. You all have decided to separate the spiritual from the physical, not realizing that the spiritual is within the physical; there is no separation. If you do one, then you also do the other. If you take one, you take the other.*

Well, except when I'm dreaming, right?

*You have a physical body of sorts, when you are dreaming. It is an ethereal physical body that is freer from gravity, has less corporeal substance than the one you have here on Earth.*

So my spirit just skips from one body to another dream body?

*It is a facsimile of your physical body. It is a lighter version of it.*

Is that similar to how I might experience different probabilities? By just changing my focus to a different probability or different physical body in a different reality?

*You can take your original physical body with you to a different reality or you can change it if you wish.*

How do I go to a different physical reality?

*You must change your state of spirituality. You must change your mind. You must change your ideas, your thoughts, especially about what is possible in your world. That will allow you to experience other realities.*

Okay, I'm going to have to think about that.

*If you have more questions about these ideas, feel free to ask. We are always happy to elaborate when things are unclear. We do not always know when you do not completely understand.*

A lot my questions have to do with time not being real. I don't right away understand all of the implications of that and it is difficult to consider them all at once.

*It may be helpful if you let the idea sit with you for a bit.*

Yes, I think that if I let it sink in then I will start to, hopefully, gain some understanding.

*Or at least some intuitive understanding if not direct conscious understanding.*

Right.

*Well, I say we have thoroughly confused you this evening.*

Yes.

*Very good.*

It is good, actually.

# CHAPTER 6
## PROBABLE SELVES AND THE NATURE OF PROBABILITIES

In this chapter Brahma and I further discuss the idea of alternate probabilities and probable selves that exist whenever we think about the decisions in our lives that take us down different paths. It's the alternate reality of what would have happened and how it is not nonexistent. It hinges on the problem of our perception of the timelines of our lives being linear, when in fact there are many branches in the paths of our past just as in those of our future.

*Good evening.*

Hello Brahma.

*It is good to be here again, my friend.*

Welcome back. Considering our last session, I still have a lot of questions regarding probabilities and time.

*Very good. We shall do our best to clarify. We are counting on you to ferret out the clarity for our readers. It is difficult to know what is clear to you when we understand all of what we are trying to convey. We need someone in your shoes to let us know what is not clearly understood*

I should be a fine candidate for playing the role of the confused reader.

*Very good!*

Okay, so along the lines of our life experience and the things that we focus on and the agreements we make, are they also related to the choices we make? I'm thinking of the choices and the decisions that we make that come up in our lives. I am always wondering about how those choices have affected my life. What are the implications of choice?

*We are unclear on the question.*

Me too.

*That explains it.*

Let me throw out an example. Say I am faced with a decision in my life and I cannot decide what I should do. It appears to me that one choice will bring me down a certain path and one choice will lead me down another completely different path. How do I know which choice I want to make?

*You do not know which choice you want to make?*

No, because I want to make both of them. In some respects I want to continue down the path I'm on and in some respects I want to continue down a new path.

*And so you travel down both paths with your consciousness and you choose one. You must. You must choose one to experience. You have nowhere to go but forward in this realm. There are alternate realities in which you can go backwards or even sideways. But in this one you must go forward and so you must make a choice. But you will, if it is important, send a probable self down the avenue you did not choose.*

A probable self?

*It is a thought form created by you which is then free to do as it chooses. It is not as complete as you at first. But it will become more solid as time continues for it.*

So it's just merely a probability?

*But the probability is a reality.*

But it seems to have diverged from my life down that road not taken?

*To you it is a probable self.*

But it is no longer a part of my experience. Correct?

*In a sense this is true, however you will receive constant communication from the self—it is your creation after all. It will convey its experience to you, you will benefit from it.*

## Probable Selves

So is that like creating a new soul-fragment?

*It is in a sense. It is a less complete soul than you are but it can become more complete. You are from the entity so you are more of a complete solidified soul when you come into this existence. If something comes from you it is one generation removed. It is like a photocopy that you continue to copy and make subsequent copies. A copy from that probable self will be even less distinct. But through choice and free will they can become more distinct if they choose, or if they do not feel they have a place they can merge back into the original energies or converge at another point on the path.*

So, the probable self is similar to a creation?

*Yes, it is like giving birth to another self through your thought prompted by your indecision. Once a choice is presented, your entity often has a need to fill both options, so in some way it must do that. You have the will to decide which option, which path you wish to follow personally, but you send some of your energy to create another self who will experience the other path.*

Okay. So when I make a decision and I move forward with the decision I have made and I am continuing down one particular path, my probable self also continues down the other path that I did not choose?

*Yes.*

So even though that other probability has a reality of its own with its own experience, is that probability in a lesser reality than the actual chosen reality that I am in?

*Its energy is not as strong to begin with. It is similar to a blueprint for a house. You are the house, the structure that has been there for many years. Then someone wishes to copy the house. So a blueprint is drawn. The blueprint will collect more thought and gain more energy and eventually will become another solid house. It starts as a less dense version, a transparency, if you will, to begin with. It may gain momentum and often does or it may fade back into your energy or into the energy of the entity if it is not strong enough or does not wish to continue on its own.*

Okay, so this other probability on this other path, say for example it is a version of me that moves on, now, does that imply that there is another reality and environment that offers experience for that other self?

*There are many layers to this reality. Or if you wish, you can think of them as alternate realities. There are countless versions of this reality in which probable selves can and do exist.*

Okay so if this reality is a co-creation between me and other energies, then for every probable self, there is also another co-created reality?

*Yes. Some of the rules in a blueprint are borrowed from your reality, but changes can be made in laws of physics and so forth in the alternate realities as well as your own.*

It seems like it would be exponentially more complicated every time someone makes a decision?

*Another reality is created, if that is what you mean. It does not necessarily make it more complicated but there are, as I mentioned, countless, countless realities just like this one. They continue to be birthed every millisecond.*

So, I exist in countless realities? Are there countless different versions of me that exist?

*Yes. You are focused only on this one. You can change your focus if you like to tap into and even perhaps experience a probable self. Or you may join one also if the desire is strong enough to move to a slightly altered version of your reality.*

So if I don't decide to access or get involved in a probable self it continues on independently and is like a copy of me living and experiencing?

*Yes.*

Now, say I were to step back from my own reality and look at my life from the point of view of my larger entity.

*Shalkeera?* [8]

Yes, now from that point of view there must be billions of Roberts to keep track of. Is it similar from your point of view as well?

---

[8] **From Chapter One, Shalkeera is the name Brahma has given us to refer to Robert's larger source entity. Shalkeera's relationship to Robert is similar to that of Brahma to Bronwen.**

## Probable Selves

*Yes, but I'm only concerned with this one Robert at the moment. However there are versions of me that speak to a few of your probable selves as well.*

Okay, let's offer an example to help clarify: Say I worked at a job with a friend and this friend of mine decides to quit his job and he goes off and gets a new job, but he still remains my friend. But there is also a probable self of his that stays working at our job. Because he made the decision to quit as well as the indecision to stay, does that obligate me to also create a probable self that maintains a friendship with him in his new job and also remain his friend in the job that we both still share? Basically, does a decision by someone else obligate my entity to create a probability as well?

*He will create a facsimile of you based on his perception of you that will exist in his probable reality. You may infuse yourself in that facsimile if you wish to experience that reality as well. It is his version of you, however. You need not focus on that probability.*

Because otherwise it would logically seem that I would be spread very thin if I had to keep track of multitudes of selves.

*You lose nothing in creation. You only add to yourself. You are more.*

But what is really more important is which probability I am focused on. Correct? Because that is the part I'm experiencing?

*You need not be part of your friend's reality unless you choose his probable self. He can create a version of you. And you need not be present.*

So do I have friends or versions of them that I have created where they are not actually there?

*Yes.*

They are just these paper stand-ins? Cardboard cutouts?

*The cardboard cutouts are from you so they also can continue on their own. But they are even less substantial to begin with than your probable self, if you can understand this: a Xerox of a Xerox. They are a creation of your probable self which is a copy of you.*

Okay.

*And the further down the line they go generation-wise, the less substantial they are. But they can become substantial, and if they become as substantial as you, then you will be a probable self to them. But this does not make you less substantial, it would only seem so from their point of view.*

So, if I am to make a critical decision and I have a probable self that is created because of my indecision, I can experience the point of view of the other decision? I'm wondering about certain times in my life when I have not really felt all the way there. Is it possible that I was just a probable self at that point?

*It is possible that you are tapping into and experiencing another self you have created. Yes. There are many places you can go during lapses of consciousness. That is one of them. You have more lapses of consciousness than you realize. It happens often. When you refocus, usually you do not recall.*

So it's possible for these other probable selves to, I guess, run out of steam if they don't pan out or seem worthwhile?

*Yes, the energy can fade back in to you or your larger entity.*

Would that be because they were never really a serious consideration?

*That is one of the possibilities, yes. It needs to have enough impetus to push it forward, and a desire to continue.*

So do these only occur when there is indecision?

*They occur whenever you think of doing something. You can create a probable self right now if you choose, walking on the beach at night in Fort Lauderdale, for example.*

I can do that with simply the desire to be there?

*Yes, by putting yourself there with the thought of it. By thinking of the situation, you will put a part of yourself there which can continue on or not. It would be good to create consciously happy selves of you in situations you would like to find yourself in because you would get happy energy from these happy creations. It is just a suggestion.*

So you are saying I can imagine myself in myriad different happy situations.

*You will place part of yourself there.*

Right, so if I put a part of my energy into those happy situations with a desire to be there, they will continue on and be available to draw upon for happy experience and good energy?

*Yes, you may draw upon them, but more likely they will just send their energy your way. You may ask them for it, but it is freely given.*

Does that work both ways, too? If a person thought of doing not-so-happy things often?

*Yes, that is correct.*

That could really bring someone down.

*Yes, that is correct. Your thoughts are more powerful than most of you realize. They do indeed create worlds.*

So all of these I'm thinking of exist more or less in the same timeline. In the last chapter, The Life Experience, we discussed the idea that I can access other selves of mine that are future selves or past selves. I understand that there are many different future selves based on what I do that are future probabilities.

*Yes.*

And last time you mentioned that there are also younger selves, young Roberts, experiencing and living, that I can also tap into. But I have to stretch my point of view because my direct experience is always focused on the now.

*Yes.*

And so these other possible experiences must be tapped into somehow or imagined?

*If you wish to, you may tap into them.*

Now, most of us have a common understanding that who we are in the present moment has a lot to do with the past that has led up to this point and the direction we are headed.

*You are a product of the* now. *Your past has influenced you, but only the past that you choose to incorporate. You can manifest or choose an alternate past if it is beneficial to you. You can do this at any time.*

Right. We discussed how I could focus on the past in a certain light and alter its effects on my present state. And can I basically do the same thing with the future?

*Yes, you can choose to follow many futures. You may choose to identify with any of myriad probable or future selves.*

So in all of these probable selves there are corresponding probable worlds with all of those?

*Yes. Think of them as multiple transparencies over your own world.*

Like in a book with transparent pages?

*Yes with slight alterations in each layer.*

So that means there are many different ways I can experience a given situation?

*Yes.*

Because to a degree, I can change who I am as I experience this and also some of the circumstances?

*Yes. The circumstances of your past and future are malleable, they are not fixed.*

So is that why people often get what they expect?

*Yes, it is a matter of focus and if someone believes they had a horrible childhood and it is holding them back, they can choose to have a childhood that was not quite so traumatic by remembering things differently.*

So, could someone do this by simply remembering happy things and forgetting the trauma?

*Or by lessening the trauma when the memory is relived. For example, one might think: "Well, I fell down the stairs when I was young and it was horrible and I now am afraid of stairs." They could instead think, "Well, I fell down the stairs but really I only bruised my knee and it wasn't so bad."*

Right, because they could think of the many other injuries they have experienced that can make falling down a few stairs seem to be quite trivial.

*Yes.*

For example, if they just think of the time they fell off the roof.

*And perhaps remembering that even that event was something they walked away from.*

Right, and if one thinks of it that way then they can change their perspective?

*More than that. One can change the course of events: one changes their past, in effect.*

One can change their past?

*One makes it so that it happened less traumatically.*

Basically what they're doing is changing the way they think of their past which then changes the effect it has on their present. Correct?

*Yes, as I mentioned, one is able to choose myriad probable pasts. They are all open. There are certain things that are embedded in the memory, certain events that would be difficult to erase. But they can be changed: [the perception of] the way they happened and their lasting effects.*

So, is there an easy way to do that? Like you explained: thinking of the past, trying to change how to feel about it and...?

*Yes, try to remember the best things about the event. Try to reshape the memory of it. When reliving it, look for the best possible scenario of that situation.*

And that can change the attitude of someone in the present?

*Yes. For example: "I fell down the stairs and scraped my knee. But I remember the stairs were actually very soft and as I came careening down, my mother was smiling at me at the foot of the stairs and ready to give me a hug and take care of me." This reshapes the event. One thinks of your mother's smiling face and the softness of the carpet.*

And so now in the future, or present, one will not be afraid of falling down stairs?

*It should improve.*

I like that. It reminds me of how sometimes hypnotism or even talking about past traumatic experiences can help see them in a different light.

*If you can identify a past event that may have caused troubles or issues that are affecting you now, it can be very helpful.*

Now, you mentioned I can create probable selves, but I imagine I have already done so. A lot of them are already created. Correct?

*Yes.*

Am I accessing those probable selves when I dream about being in other lives?

*Many times, you are.*

Maybe, for example, if I am having recurring dreams?

*Yes. Dreams of a past self who still continues.*

Is there a way to consciously access these other selves, these other experiences?

*You have only to concentrate upon it.*

So is it just easier in dreams because of my state of mind?

*Yes, that is correct. But you can do it consciously. Many of you censor your thoughts when you are conscious. It is the ego that is largely responsible for this censoring. You imagine an other self and you imagine things happening to this self. Your imaginings are a true reflection. They are real. But your ego says, "No, I am the only one. These are just flights of fancy." And it convinces you that you are not glimpsing any truth. And you think you are having silly thoughts.*

Why does the ego do that?

*The ego feels threatened. It does not wish to see its larger self. These probable selves also have their own egos, you see.*

So the ego is necessarily narrow-minded?

*Yes, very much so. It was created this way out of necessity. It is, as I have said, still being refined.*

But it helps one focus in this reality. Right?

*Yes, it is very important for the intensity of the earthly experience to have a very strong focus.*

So it is like a microscope.

*Yes.*

It sees very well but only in a narrow field of view.

*Yes, very well and very narrow.*

Is that the only way one can fully focus on this narrow point of view?

*That is correct. At the time.*

But one does not always have to perceive things through the ego. Right?

*You can try to get around it. You can tell it to be quiet when it tells you, "You are just imagining things". You can disagree with it.*

So is that like what one might do during meditation?

*Meditation is an emptying of the mind which in effect does try to put aside the ego for a time.*

Like going to sleep?

*Yes, you do not take your ego with you when you sleep. You are in another dimension, the ego cannot follow.*

So one just has to put the ego to sleep, in a way?

*Yes, essentially. Or, as I said, you can disagree with your ego or you can try to stretch your ego. Try to get your ego to believe, to understand.*

If one stretched their ego to consider existing in other realities, couldn't that be very confusing and possibly cause mental disorders?

*Only in extreme cases. But if you are mentally stable and you work on stretching your ego gently, this will not likely occur. If you use a gateway mechanism such as drugs like LSD, this can cause mental problems and instability. That is not a gentle stretching of the ego. It is a very harsh one and can cause instability in the personality. It does not always do this. Some people can handle this, but it is not recommended. When you use this drug you may be experiencing alternate realities and probable selves but you take your ego with you. This can be very hard on it. It is often like a scared child. You must be gentle with it so that it does not freak out.*

So I need to take care of my ego?

*Yes, be gentle. But it is good to stretch it a bit if you can.*

Right. So in regard to these probable selves, the best I can get from the experience is just sort of a glimpse into that experience. Is it possible to have a more intense focus on a probable self?

*You can actually become the probable self. You can merge with it if that is your desire.*

Can I do that and then come back?

*Yes. But it has to work in this reality along a logical chain of events. Let us say for instance, you no longer wish to be in your current occupation, but you instead wish to work again at your previous job. There is a probable self of yours that never quit that job and is still working there. You would have to quit your job and apply again at your old job. At some point you would find yourself in a position comparable to what you previously had when you quit. This position would be comparable to the one your probable self holds. You have effectively merged with a probable self. Now, let us suppose you decided that this situation wasn't for you after all. You could apply again to your current job and work again at your current occupation. There would be minor differences such as a loss in seniority or pay but the reality would be the same and yet altered.*

Okay.

*It needs to follow a logical path, generally speaking. Although, there are times when you can wake up in an alternate reality with things slightly altered. Some of these things do not make logical sense, but in small leaps these things are often ignored or reasoned away.*

So someone can make small leaps from one probability to another?

*Yes.*

Just not major ones because the problem is the drastic change in logical consistency?

*Yes. There was a book that Bronwen had accidentally given away. She searched for it high and low, to no avail. One morning she woke up and knew exactly where it would be. This was a side step into an alternate reality where she had not given away the book. But the reality was so similar to her own this was only a minor change.*

Just the one thing was changed not anything else major?

*Yes.*

So is that why things like time travel aren't really practical? Is it because it is too drastic of a change of reality?

*It cannot be explained to the ego. But there may come a time when it is feasible when man has developed a logical explanation. When it is believable, it is possible.*

That makes sense. So there are other probabilities out there but it's not likely that another probable self would cross back into this reality, is it?

*Yes, it is not likely.*

But is it possible? Can I run into myself?

*You would not very often run into yourself. If two probabilities wound up in the same reality, they would merge. It can happen. It does not happen very often.*

So it could actually happen? Maybe that is what happens when I effectively alter my past. By remembering a situation and focusing on different aspects of it that I didn't focus on before and effectively changing my memory of it…

*…you can merge with a probable self.*

So using the example of the traumatic fall on a stairway, there is a probable self that grew up completely unafraid of falling down stairs. Changing the reaction to the memory and eliminating the fear has the same result of merging with that probable self?

*Yes. There are realities in which there are very few things that are changed. There are also realities where many large things are changed. But there are enough realities that have small changes that are close to you that you can merge with them fairly easily without too many steps.*

Okay.

*I hope it is a little clearer now. I understand this is a confusing issue for linear thinkers such as you.*

It is confusing but the more I think about it, the more sense it makes. Trying to open my mind to the possibility seems to help.

*Yes. That is the preferred method.*

Perhaps I could alter my past a little bit so that I understand better?

*You may do that.*

So I do not have such a narrow point of view.

*Yes, you can always expand your viewpoint, your world view. It is usually helpful to do so.*

Yes, I agree. It seems to allow for more happiness.

*Yes, and it brings more understanding and more interesting experience.*

---

Okay. Now, you mentioned lapses of consciousness earlier in this chapter where one could be possibly tapping into and experiencing other selves.

*Yes. Or other realities.*

Or other realities, yes. Now, it seems to me that as I live my life, and from birth to death, it seems as though I would have more experiences and more decisions and more probabilities as I progress along this life. At this point it seems as though there are lots of other paths that I could have gone down, and each of those paths having more branching paths as well. There are so many choices I could have made.

*They are choices that you did make.*

Right. Okay, yes, in a way all choices were made. Now, given that there are so many branches and probabilities later in life and that at times I could be focused on them and even participating in these alternate probabilities, does that explain certain lapses of consciousness? Specifically, is that why, as I get older, I seem to have more lapses of consciousness? Also, as I get older it seems as though the passage of time goes by quicker? Is that because I'm spending more of my time in other realities and in other probabilities?

*You are growing spiritually and time does seem to progress more quickly as you age.*

Yes, it does.

*You are busier because you have discovered that there are other realms in which you can play, so you send parts of yourselves off to play and dance in these other realms and to create in them. You spend part of your time doing this and you come back with your consciousness to your body and you say, "oh my, look how much time has passed!" And you are busier than you were. You are more creative as you continue along the path.*

Right, and my experience in it is fuller?

*Yes, you are doing more and, therefore, to you it appears as though more time has passed because space and time are related, interconnected, and if you have done all this extra stuff, more time must have passed. You have skipped around in space, and time must have elapsed also from your perspective.*

Does that explain attention deficit disorder? People focusing on other things all the time. Are we multitasking probable selves?

*You most certainly are doing this, yes. Some of you more than others. Attention deficit disorder is very much the playing in other realities by the consciousness. It is also a slightly underdeveloped ego that does not have the tenacity to stick to this particular earth environment. So, off consciousness goes playing in these other realms without paying as much attention to the one at hand, specifically the particular focus of the consciousness that most of you have here in this earthly realm, this physical reality.*

Okay. Another question about probabilities. We talked about probable selves and how a lot of them were created when I made decisions in my life. It seems possible and I would like to ask if it is. Can I just go back in my mind and remember a situation and think, "Aha, I just thought of a better way of doing that," and create a new probability retroactively?

*Yes, the past is as plastic as the future. There are many pasts and many futures from which to choose but now is the point of power. If you decide now that there is a better past for you, you can go back and change it and live from now, having been there and made this decision or proceeded on this path that you have now decided you should have or could have walked upon.*

Okay. So the probability doesn't have to have been made at the time of the decision?

*Absolutely not. You see, time is plastic [easily molded or shaped] as well.*

So, in a sense it is like the future. Would that be analogous to, "I think next week I will make a decision and of one of those decisions I will make two other decisions" and they are all still possible or even probable depending on which way I direct my attention?

*Yes, there are many possibilities.*

And you are saying that I can do that to the past as well?

*Absolutely.*

So is that the same thing as changing my past?

*Yes. If you decide you should have done something differently and you start to remember it that way, then you have effectively changed your past. The only personal importance of any past event is how it affects the present.*

Because you mentioned that it is possible to merge with a probable self.

*Yes, these probable selves in their probable realities are all around you. They are close by.*

But changing the past seems to be less confusing than merging with a probability.

*It is the same thing, in essence.*

We used the example of a person who is afraid of falling down stairs and trying to remember the incident that caused that in a different light, thereby changing the probability of the person existing with a fear of falling down stairs or not.

*Yes.*

By changing the past, it seems like I can change that and I can remember something positive that came out of that, and then I am effectively changing my past because I am changing what I brought with me to my present.

*Yes, to the point of now.*

Yes, that makes sense to me. It seems more difficult or confusing to think of both probabilities with one probability being the person who is afraid of falling down stairs and the other probability being one who is not and both continuing their lives. It seems as though many things all along the way would be different, and to merge with that would almost be like having to change all of the path.

*In order to merge with either probability, you must change something from your past.*

But can you change just one thing?

*Yes, there are multitudes, millions upon millions of probabilities. Some are very close to your own and some have dramatic changes. Yes, you can change one small thing.*

Even physical things?

*Such as?*

Well, mental things seem easy. A psychological problem seems like it would be easy to fix, relatively.

*Yes.*

But what about one that resulted in a physical injury?

*This can be changed as well depending upon the severity of the injury.*

I mean, it is easy for me to think, "Well, gosh, I could have lost my finger in that incident but I didn't. I still have my finger."

*Yes.*

But it seems difficult to say, "Oh, I could have kept my finger."

*It is probable. It is possible, shall we say, to wake up with a newly attached finger and remember the rest of it—losing the finger—as a dream. It is possible.*

So it would just become like some bad nightmare?

*Yes, this would most likely occur, if it were going to occur, after a good night of sleep. It would not suddenly appear in your waking reality. The other reality would have to be remembered as a dream.*

But it would have to be an entirely new reality, not just a change of my person?

*Or a new probability, you in a different probability.*

Which comes with all new people?

*It may or it may not come with new people. There are many probabilities, some very close to your own and some very far away. You can just change one small thing. I am repeating this.*

Okay, yes. In each, reality would have an agreement of all of the people in it of what happened?

*Yes, naturally. Although there will always be slightly different versions.*

Right, slightly different versions because of different perspectives?

*Yes, but a general agreement would be reached. There might be someone amongst your friends who says, "I thought you lost that finger in the fire," and everyone else will say, "No, no, silly, he almost lost it. But as you can see, the finger is fine." This sort of thing can occur.*

Okay. So, each different probability may have overlapping aspects and that is why some people remember things incorrectly. It is because in some nearby probability, they are actually correct.

*Yes. I know this is difficult to comprehend from your point of view while you are actually focused on only one present probability.*

Right, it is difficult to understand what my house looks like while I am always inside it.

*You must open your mind to imagine how your house looks to me.*

Now, probable selves can be the result of the different directions I could go in any decision, and each has its own corresponding reality with other people in it. Right?

*Yes, that is correct.*

Now, with this in mind, other people perceiving me in different ways can also create other probabilities of me. So if somebody has a mistaken perception of me, can that create a probable self of me that is different than how I actually am?

*This is correct. This is also why when people think well of you and they encourage you, this can propel you into a probable self that is more successful and perhaps more desirable to you.*

Is that because these other probabilities have some sort of effect on me?

*Yes. Now you can choose to accept or reject other people's perception of you, of course.*

I can? Can I just say, "That is not me," and be unaffected?

*Yes, say, "I do not accept this probability or perception of me," and then you will not be swayed by it.*

I can see that this may be easy if one person has an undesirable opinion of me. But what if there was an overwhelming number of people who are looking at me in a certain light because of some huge rumor that has been spread about me?

*If your self-will is strong enough you will not be affected by it. If everyone says you cannot run a 4-minute mile and you truly believe that you can, then you will be able to do so.*

Okay. But if I wanted to accept this other probability or perception, I could. Right? It can help me in the same way. Right? If someone believes I am a great leader and I have my doubts, can their perception help me?

*Yes, if you choose to accept their belief in you, it can propel you forward.*

But I must accept it?

*Yes, it is not just all what you believe. It is what you believe, but it is also what you accept, if you accept the energy coming from these others or not.*

Okay. So, as practical advice it would be good to rely a lot on what I believe about myself when it is good and to be judicious in what I accept about what others think about me?

*This is correct. Now, younger souls or those not as schooled in doing this can unconsciously accept things because they do not realize what they are accepting. Good or bad thoughts about them can affect them more than those who are more conscious of such things or who are older or more experienced with such things. Energies do affect you, you see, and the more experience you have with being affected or not affected by energies, the more you will be the master of your own destiny.*

So, simply thinking about another person in a certain way is offering energy to them that can have an affect them?

*Yes. And they can accept or reject this according to their skill level and their desire.*

So from an ethical point of view, I should be looking for and thinking about only the greatest aspects of everyone?

*We do not know about it being ethical or not, however this would be the most beneficial to you and all other energies.*

So, it would not be beneficial to think of another person in a poor light?

*This is correct. It is not beneficial to you or to this other person.*

But it is not necessarily harmful?

*It could be, but not necessarily. This is correct. Each spiritual energy or personality will choose to accept or reject it, or it will not be skilled enough and will just accept it like a gullible child.*

Is that why we like it when other people think highly of us?

*Yes, it gives us an energy boost if we choose to accept it, and most people will try to accept this type of energy.*

So we do get something out of having other people thinking highly of us?

*Yes.*

Thank you for shedding some light on probabilities. I see that it is not as simple as I thought.

*It will likely become clearer if you let it sink in.*

Thank you for this lesson on probabilities.

*Thank you for listening.*

# CHAPTER 7
## THE DEATH EXPERIENCE

In this chapter, we discuss some of what actually happens when we die. We learn how our body and mind consciousnesses are affected by death as opposed to dreaming or lapses in consciousness or states of unconsciousness like seizures, shock, and comas. We see how our expectations affect our initial experience in death, and Brahma sheds some light on the feelings that one has as they die toward those that they leave behind who are mourning.

---

*We are at your service.*

Hello Brahma.

*Hello my friend.*

Welcome back.

*Why, thank you. We are very pleased to be in your presence this evening. Thank you for allowing us this opportunity.*

You are always welcome. So, we have talked about the nature of the soul and dreams and reincarnation and we have discussed how the soul continues on after we die, after we cross over.

*Yes.*

Let's talk about the actual death experience, the point where the consciousness of the body and the soul separate.

*Yes.*

Now I also believe we described it as sort of a reunion, a turning inward, a reunion with the larger entity.

*Yes, the eternal energy of the soul.*

Yes, the soul being the larger entity or collection of soul-fragments. Now, to many of us this seems like a pretty big transition.

*Yes. It would seem that way to you from a linear, single-soul based perspective, the perspective with which you now are focused in physical reality. However the larger part of you doesn't see it as a big deal. Just another fly landing on your shoulder which you shrug off, if you understand.*

Yes. Now, my understanding is that our problem with death has to do with our ego or body consciousness. Is that why death seems like something to be feared?

*Yes, the ego, as you know from chapter two, has been constructed in order to facilitate your experience in this realm of reality. The ego is a part of you that you have created. It is something temporary, something that dies, in a way, when you cross over. It does not retain the same identity that you retain. Your ego does not come with you when you sleep and dream, and you know this because you notice there is a part of yourself that is often uncensored and unafraid. The censoring part of your personality, the scared part of your personality, is largely due to the ego. When you are in the dream state or you are not connected to the ego, you can sense this freedom. Sometimes you have trouble going to sleep because the ego does not wish to let go. But when you wake up the next morning, the ego realizes it is still there. When you cross over it will still be there, in a way. But in a way, it will not be there. It has a type of death that is difficult to explain.*

So it's not a death in the way we're talking about the death experience, it's more kind of just being set aside, or put on hold, or turned off?

*Yes, the part of you that was the ego remains but it no longer has a job. And so it is dormant.*

Okay. Yeah, you mentioned before that it was sort of a tool that we use. It functions as a contractor would in managing the building of a house.

*Yes.*

And when it no longer has a job it is sort of set aside. It is an unemployed contractor. Correct?

*Yes. It does not wish to be without a function. It is somewhat of a control freak.*

The ego is a control freak?

*Yes.*

I assume that is an inherent requirement and it is necessary for it to function the way that it does?

*Yes. As I said, it is the best we have right now for allowing experience to come from this realm into the more eternal.*

Right.

*We desire this because we are hungry for experience. It is like watching the next episode of a beloved television show. You can't wait to see what happens next.*

Right. Okay, I guess a lot of the fear of death that we have is largely due to the ego. But some people's concern is that it is going to hurt.

*Yes.*

Here is my next question: Is death painful?

*It depends upon the individual. Many times the personality will leave the body before pain is experienced. However there are some personalities that wish to, or feel like they must, experience the pain along with the death. And so there are some who remain in their bodies until the very last moment. It is, perhaps, about 50/50, as you say. There are some personalities that leave the body weeks or months before the passing and they do not even perceive this. Those who are senile or have Alzheimer's often have already left. They might check in once in a while, but for all intents and purposes they have departed this life.*

So that seems to be contrary to some of the ideas I've heard about, for example when there is a story about a soul that is confused because it doesn't know that it's dead.

*This can occur, of course.*

But is it often the other way around? For example, that a soul doesn't realize it is still living?

*Sometimes this can happen if you are speaking of the symptoms of Alzheimer's disease.*

Yes. That is what I was thinking about. So the situation can be such that someone doesn't realize that they still have a functioning body here.

*Yes. Sometimes the body consciousness continues on with only an occasional look-in from the soul-fragment, from the spirit.*

Does it happen sometimes that a soul will pass on or have the death experience and not really be aware of that, be confused and somehow stay around this reality?

*Yes, this is not the rule, but rather the exception. It can happen but it doesn't often. Most of the time when people experience what you like to call hauntings or ghosts, usually these are just energy impressions. However, there are occasions where a personality will not realize they are dead in your terms and they are confused and do not know where to turn despite the pleadings of guides all around them asking them to look, to see. They will sometimes ignore this, they will not see it. But as I said, this is more the exception than the rule. Most of the time when one crosses over, there will be an immediate recognition and a sort of "aha moment", you see. A sort of awakening.*

Now, regarding ghosts or hauntings, usually they are just energy impressions. But is it possible that the ego or body consciousness can remain after the soul-fragment leaves?

*Yes. But as I said before, the ego has a sort of death when it is no longer employed by the soul-fragment.*

So the mind consciousness leaves with the soul-fragment and the cellular consciousness goes about decomposing or whatever biological process is appropriate for them.

*That is correct.*

Can I assume that the ego, with no direction from the soul, will just dissipate?

*Yes, without a job to do, it does just that.*

With its strong survival instinct, could it sometimes linger about without the body?

*Yes, this is possible. It may be particularly stubborn in accepting its unemployment and can attempt to assemble energetically a form like it had before. This form may resemble the body of the person it was involved with. However, without the soul or mind consciousness, the cellular consciousness of the body will not cooperate. The ego or body consciousness will only be able to temporarily manipulate fluid molecules like molecules of air. The effect is fleeting but would account for some ghost sightings.*

Regarding the death experience, I guess the nearest thing I can personally compare it to is my dream experience?

*Yes.*

Am I to understand that in this death experience there is an awakening that is different than in the dream experience?

*It would be most similar to those who can awaken in their dreams as in lucid dreaming. It is most similar to this in terms of your earthly experience.*

Okay. Because a lot of my dreams, when I can remember them, seem to be foggy or perhaps, dreamy.

*Yes, in lucid dreaming there is an enhanced perception of feeling, of color, of vitality which even exceeds the vitality you feel here on earth most of the time. It is a super-awakening. There is no fatigue. There is enhanced perception.*

Okay, no fogginess, no drowsiness.

*This is most often not the case. It would perhaps be similar to a drug experience where one was feeling super-real, if that makes any sense to you.*

Yes, it does. So it's more vivid than the typical dream state?

*Yes. Yes. And if you woke up in your dreams you could experience this more vivid reality.*

Okay.

*But you have your conscious mind with you which does not die. And you often leave your conscious mind in your body when you dream, but you can take it with you, with practice. If not, when you have the death experience, you will suddenly be thrust into this world with your conscious mind. And you will be very surprised and unpracticed. Not that this is cause for alarm. Some adapt easily. Others have a few troubles.*

Is that because of lack of practice or because of the belief systems that they have?

*Many times it is because of lack of belief or some conflicting beliefs that preclude the experience that you are having. If you do not believe that there is life after life, you could feel nothing for a very long time. Or you could be extremely confused that there was something afterward. Or if you believe that there will be an eternal heaven or an eternal hell, the reality that you will find yourself in will reflect that. Hopefully you will believe that you are worthy of heaven in this case. However you will quickly tire of such a scenario of sitting on the clouds and playing harps. And there will be guides who will be attempting to awaken you from your dream-within-the-dream to the true reality. That being that <u>you</u> are the creator of your experience and of the heaven or hell that you are experiencing. There is no god with a white beard looking over you. There is no eternal authority.*

So a heaven or a hell that one might find themselves in is purely of their own creation?

*Yes. But you may borrow from others creations. If you have read Dante's Inferno perhaps you will experience some of that, for example (Brahma is laughing here). Thank you, Dante, for the poetic misinformation!*

So, I am assuming that we get to bring with us the knowledge and experience that we've had in this life.

*Yes, of course.*

Do we become more enlightened? After we die, do we find out things we did not know?

*You will re-merge with your energy, your multiple energy which is more than you. You will then be able to experience and know all that your entity knows, and, additionally, you will experience the feelings and thoughts of every one you have connected with during your lifetime: Things that you may not know, ways that you affected people that you may not realize, even ways that you have affected the earth that you are largely unaware of.*

So we would have access to that information? I'm assuming we would also have more access to other knowledge that we didn't have any direct contact with.

For example, would we have access to what Socrates was thinking when he was here?

*If you chose to tap into his worldview, you could have access to his thoughts. The [concept of] worldview has been mentioned by other teachers. It is an energy imprint, a way of thinking. Each of you leaves behind, or continues depending on how you see it, a worldview which can be tapped into by others. It is a way of being, a way of thinking. In essence you can put your mind into this worldview of someone else and understand their worldview.*

So there are no secrets in heaven?

*(Laughing) There is no heaven my friend unless you make it! You may make a heaven if you choose. But yes, beyond this reality there are no secrets. There is no need for such things. You are very much focused on deception and lies in order to cover things up or not hurt someone's feelings. There is no need for this in the other realm. Feelings cannot be hurt. If someone does not like you, you simply move on. It is not a hurtful thing. There is no deception.*

So getting our feelings hurt would be something we experience only in this reality?

*Yes.*

Is it an ego thing?

*Yes, it is very much connected to the ego, especially the ego that thinks it must be in control at all times.*

And so without that there is no worry of hurting someone else's feelings?

*There is an eternal love that most tap into. The universe was created with this feeling of love. I do not speak of love in terms of the sentiment. I speak of love in terms of the force that propels the universe. It is not a sentimental thing. It is a force of greatness, and you are surrounded by this. Many feel this force of love when they cross over. If someone does not like you and you are surrounded by love, it does not hurt you. If you are surrounded by a chorus of people who say, "I love you, I love you, I love you," and someone walks out from far away and crosses the street toward you and says, "I do not love you," and there are hundreds of people loving you, you will not really feel it. You will say, "Alright then go to who you love. I am loved. I need nothing more."*

Okay. Interesting.

Many people who have had near-death experiences have reported that they hover above their body and their soul is rising up out of it or even looking down from above. We always have this perception of people rising upwards after death. Is that just because of a belief system or does this kind of thing really happen as you die?

*It depends upon the individual but it is certainly possible to rise up out of your body and observe. It is just an advantageous viewpoint to observe the situation. One thing that seems interesting to most of you when you have this experience at death or near-death is that you see it very objectively and you are not used to this feeling. You might look down on your body in a hospital while they are working on it while someone is crying over you and you see it all with sort of a detached interest. You, might say, "Oh, they are working on me. I am dying. Oh, that person is very sad. Oh, this is so interesting." And the detachment is also very surprising to you. The reason you feel this detachment is because you have a sudden knowing that everything is alright. You feel that everyone continues, that every personality and every love that you've ever had is not lost but continues. You do not feel loss. This allows you to see wars and turmoil going on below you and you can see it with detached interest. Compassion can accompany this, but it is not compassion in the way that you often think of it. The compassion that Bronwen often has for animals, for example, is an attached compassion. There is another type of compassion that is detached and is less painful to the perceiver, if you can understand what I'm trying to get across.*

There is a detached compassion?

*Yes. There is a love, but a knowing that all will be well, and as you are seeing someone suffer you see them also as whole, you see them as complete and you know that they will be well.*

So there is caring but there is not emotional concern or pity or feeling sorry for them?

*There is no pity. There is no feeling sorry for. That is correct. And we try, as teachers, to encourage you not to do that for others in this life. We would encourage you not to have pity for others because it is useless and in some ways a little bit insulting, because they are whole. You are just failing to see them this way.*

I can see how that would be insulting if you are really only looking at a small portion of their existence and assuming that they can't handle a situation.

*Yes, that is correct. Their larger self can handle it even if a part of them is suffering. And you do them no service to pity them. But seeing them as whole and healthy will help them. Do what you can to help, but do not pity them. That is our advice. Do what you wish, of course.*

We seem to have a lot of compassion sometimes for the suffering of others. In regards to compassion and pity, if it could be insulting to pity others, should we still pursue things like the prevention of the suffering of others?

*If it is within your power to prevent it, it is good to do what you can because the suffering, although there is no need to pity it, is actually your suffering on some level. It is a part of the greater entity of the greater entity of the greater entity that includes you and is essentially you. By helping others to heal their suffering and their wounds you are in a way, healing yourself.*

So is that why it hurts to see others suffering?

*Yes. It is you and you are aware that it is you on some level.*

So how is it then that people can inflict pain and suffering on others without compassion?

*They are not aware. They do not know what they do. They do not understand the full extent of their actions.*

That doesn't seem like a good enough reason for some of the cruelty in this world: to just not know. We don't let people off the hook because they are unaware of some laws.

*Well, you forgive a cat for playing with a mouse before killing it, do you not?*

Yes.

*A cat does not understand the suffering that is involved for the mouse. And you forgive the cat for this reason.*

Is that because it doesn't understand, or maybe because it doesn't have the capacity to understand?

*It does not have the capacity to understand. That is correct, at this time. Now, we hope that eventually those who inflict suffering will grow and at some point will have the capacity to understand what they're doing and therefore, stop. But until then they are like children or cats playing with mice. They have no understanding of the reality of the situation. They do not understand that they are also the mouse, you see.*

Yes, that helps. So it's important to consider the perpetrator's capacity for understanding. I'm not sure if that's enough to forgive all transgressions, especially since it is hard to know how much others can understand.

Tell me more about the death experience, the actual transition.

*The death experience is very different for different people. Some will experience pain and some will experience nothing. Many will be surprised and many pleasantly so. There is often the tunnel. This is a symbolic transition from one plane of existence to another and some will see the tunnel and be drawn to it. Some will see the light. Many of us larger entities think of ourselves as creatures of light. And so therefore going to the light is symbolic with the joining with us—we who are the larger eternal souls. Some will be confused and afraid, but there will always be guides waiting to help explain.*

*Because [with] each soul [who is] is a newly minted soul, there is no former death experience for comparison. There will be no feeling of having done this before except after you have connected with your entity. When you have connected with your entity you will realize you have done this before. But for your single personality-fragment, your soul-fragment, when you are still feeling separate, when you are still feeling like the small you, there will be no previous experience. So your entity and friends of your entity will always send those who will try to help you, try to explain to you what is happening, to try to cushion you against the shock should there be one. Although, some will need no such cushioning. Some will become vibrantly alive and very pleased and will have many things to do, many personalities to re-encounter and to share with.*

We are trying to consider what many think of as a death experience as a comparison. We are hoping you can supply us with some more possibilities of what people commonly believe.

Okay. The tunnel was a common example. So, when someone has the death experience, does their whole life flash before their eyes?

*In a sense it does. Some people experience this in a literal way and some people experience this in a more figurative way. It is an immediate knowing of everything that you have ever done and every one you have ever touched. It is what some call a life review and it can happen in a millisecond. You can become aware of everything in the smallest iota of time. That is, everything you have done, everyone you have touched and how you have affected them. You will be aware of all of the consequences of all of your actions be they for better or for worse.*

So, can this type of thing happen when people have a near-death experience and they come back?

*Yes. Many at this point, if they have died and there is the opportunity to come back, have a choice, and they can continue into the realms of light to join us, or they can go back for more experience. Many times there is an option in this case. In the case of many of the near-death experiences that you have heard about, many times there was not necessarily an intention to return, just an option. Does this make sense?*

Yes, so one can basically die and have some of the death experiences where there is life review and even some of the reconnection with the larger entity. At some point they can still come back but only if there is an option to return. It's not just because there is desire or strong will. Correct?

*Yes.*

Is there a point where they go too far and cannot come back?

*In a sense, this sometimes occurs. When you go far enough there is such a feeling of reunion and love that many times it is very, very difficult to return. This is because there is such a feeling of lightness and joy in most cases, and your body and your earthly experience feel so heavy and difficult by comparison. So in a sense, yes, it is willpower, very strong willpower that is needed at such a point. However, sometimes there are earthly connections that can draw you back from even beyond this even if you really, really don't want to return. If you have a child for instance that is counting on you then perhaps you will find the strength to return.*

Could it depend on how much happiness one has had in their life in comparison when they feel the heavy burden to go back?

*It always feels like a burden to go back. But sometimes there is a desire to do something that must be done. You might feel incomplete. You might say, "There is one more thing that I would really like to get done in this life and I have this opportunity to go back and do it, and it is hard but I really must do this thing."*

Okay. Then incomplete lives and connections with other people can draw someone back?

*Yes, if they're strong enough.*

Now, there are some people who think that one just dies, that's it, and there is no afterlife.

*Yes, and for those people, some of them will experience nothing for a long period of time despite the behest of their guides. And some will be surprised and they will immediately perceive their reality. They may be pleasantly surprised, or perhaps mortified depending upon the personality.*

You mean maybe they were hoping for nothing and being wrong is worse than being eternal?

*(Laughing) Many who hope for oblivion are not pleased! Although, there are not many of you that hope for such a thing. Some hope for this because of their pain in life. They may expect that any existence will be painful. The pain upon death, if there is any pain, will subside, of course. As soon as the spirit has had enough of this, it will disengage itself from the body. It will leave the body. The body may show outward signs of being in pain, but many times the spirit will have already left.*

So, the pain only comes from the consciousness of the body?

*Yes, it is the body consciousness and it is the connection to it that causes pain. That's why the spirit will escape when it no longer wishes to experience this or no longer feels that it must. There are some personalities that like to feel every nitty-gritty emotion and pinprick, and there are others that shy away from such things and do not wish for this experience. Now, Bronwen, for example, believes that she does not wish to experience any pin pricks or pain at all and yet she is fascinated by such things on some level and so she tortures herself a little at times.*

Is this because she doesn't want to experience pain when she dies?

*She doesn't. But, as I said, she does in a way. There is a fascination with pain and so she will sometimes call it to her without realizing it. Sort of a morbid fascination like with a car wreck. She doesn't want it but she can't help but be drawn to the sensation at times.*

So it is the connection to the body consciousness that causes the sensation of pain?

*Yes, this is correct.*

And therefore, after we die, we will have no ability to feel pain?

*That is correct.*

I'm curious about how this actually works. What happens then when we experience what we refer to as shock, when we are obviously injured and yet are feeling no pain?

*In this case, there is a disconnect of belief. The body consciousness does feel the pain on some level, but the soul does not yet believe that the injury has occurred. So there is a delayed reaction. Now in purely scientific physical terms, according to your scientists and doctors, it is a protective mechanism of the body. However this does not discount the fact that there is also a spiritual disconnect or a type of disbelief.*

Okay. So it is a delayed reaction. Does that mean that later I'm going to experience the pain?

*Yes, when the consciousness accepts that the injury has occurred. It is sort of a shock of the spirit as well.*

Okay. Now scientifically, it could be said that it works a lot like anesthesia. When somebody is unconscious they feel no pain. Is that explained by the brain consciousness not being connected to the body consciousness?

*In this case, the mind consciousness is not connected with the body consciousness. Not fully. The spirit sort of jumps into the watcher position for that short span of time and looks at what is going on, but is not directly experiencing it because it is in a slight state of temporary disbelief until it can wrap its mind around the reality that has occurred. Spirit does not always like sudden injuries and needs time to process, however briefly, depending upon the personality. Not all personalities will experience shock for every injury. You see, if you have a major injury there is a need to restructure the personality. It takes a bit of time and effort to re-frame and rebuild.*

So you're saying that the spirit is not connected in belief? It makes sense to me that when someone is unconscious that they would not feel the pain because their consciousness is off somewhere else in dreamland. But when they're fully conscious, there is disconnect?

*But you are not fully in your body if you are in shock. You are partially in the watcher position watching it as though it is happening to someone else and yet it is you. You know this but cannot yet believe it.*

So it is as if I have my body consciousness but not my spirit, my mind consciousness?

*A portion of your spirit lifts out of your body temporarily during such an event. It is as though it is surprised or shocked out of the body temporarily. Not all of your spirit, just a portion of it. And that is the portion that helps you connect to the feeling part of your physicality, the sensory part of your physicality. You can be partially in your body at any time. There are moments when you stare off into space and you come back and you ask, "Where was I?" You were partially projecting out of your body. You were not all there. People will sometimes tease others by saying, "You're not all there right now," and this is not only figuratively true, but it is also literally true. Part of your consciousness is elsewhere. This is not uncommon. You project part of your consciousness out many times during the day while still retaining your day to day functioning self.*

Okay. I never considered that. I just assumed that when I am awake I'm here and when I'm asleep I'm not.

*It can be scientifically measured, if I have not mentioned it before. You have heard of grand mal seizures, yes?*

Yes.

*These are the seizures experienced by what you call epileptics. But everyone has petite mal seizures. These are sort of an emptiness of the brain. The two hemispheres do not seem connected, briefly, and electrical activity will be similar to that of an epileptic experiencing a grand mal seizure, only it may take only a millisecond to a few seconds. These are projections of your consciousness into other realms. Your state of shock is similar to this.*

So it's a consciousness disconnect?

*Yes, very briefly. However briefly, until the personality can assimilate what has occurred to them.*

So, it is a temporary brief disconnect between the spiritual consciousness and the body consciousness?

*Between the mind and the body consciousness. Sometimes people will project all of their consciousness out. This happens often in instances such as car accidents.*

You mean the mind consciousness is projected out?

*Consciousness will project completely out of the body, and the mind will watch the event occurring and never connect to the body consciousness. Now, at this point the mind consciousness can leave for good or return when the body is in the hospital being treated, for instance.*

Right. So when you say the mind consciousness, what are you are referring to?

*What you think of as you. What you refer to when you use the term 'I'.*

Right. So it's the mental and spiritual consciousness, the part of me that goes off in dreams and is also here when I'm awake.

*Yes. The soul-fragment.*

And who is the leader of this group of consciousness that I have?

*Just the soul-fragment.*

So the mind consciousness is the soul-fragment?

*Yes. Not to be confused with the personality fragment, which is the soul-fragment incarnate and includes the molecular, body and mind consciousness.*

Right. Okay.

*But it could also be thought of as a spiritual event as well.*

Of course.

*Sometimes in a predator-prey relationship, although the prey appears to be suffering and struggling, it has already left its body consciousness and the body consciousness is the only consciousness struggling with the pain, not the soul of the prey.*

Right. Because that may not be a part of the experience they want to have?

*That is correct. Yes. Sometimes the personality sees the occurrence and does not wish to believe it, or does not wish to experience it, but it is too far drawn into it to retreat completely and so it retreats temporarily. If you break your arm and you believe that you have broken it even if you do not want to experience it, if you believe it, you have probably gone too far down the path to avoid experiencing the full effects of this.*

Right. So it's not possible to indefinitely maintain a disconnect?

*Not unless you decide to cross over.*

Right, without just dying. Eventually, if you come back you're going to have to deal with the pain.

*Yes.*

Okay. Except if you go into a coma perhaps?

*Perhaps, although some of those who have gone into a coma have actually crossed over.*

Right.

*Not all of them. Not those who are deciding to return.*

So, during the death experience and even during life-threatening experiences, we experience a form of shock that can be referred to as being the disconnect between the body consciousness and the mind consciousness or soul-fragment consciousness and this is why we feel no pain.

*Yes, that is correct.*

---

Many times when we see someone close to us who is dying, we feel like they are abandoning us. How true is this?

*In a sense they are abandoning you.*

So they are just going off to be with their happy selves in the afterlife?

*Yes.*

And leaving us here, alone?

*Yes. In a sense they are doing this. However they do often hover about and they try to give you their energy. Many times if you have a close relationship, they will support you from the other side.*

So they can still send us energy somehow?

*Yes. They can send you their energy and love and support. So although you do not perceive them, they will often be involved in your lives.*

Okay. It is good to know that they are not completely gone and I think many people will find this reassuring.

---

Now, why do some people not believe that souls continue on after death?

*You are free to believe whatever you wish. People sometimes want the experience of lacking belief. They want to be totally enclosed in this physical world. They want to experience it as if it were the only reality, the only thing that means anything: something purely physical. Something purely material. One way to do that is to incorporate a lack of belief in anything but the physical world. It can be a conscious choice of the soul-fragment. It can also be forgetfulness on the part of the ego.*

Right.

*Sometimes those who create realities that are less than they desire, including one bad thing after another bad thing happening in their lives, may decide also not to believe because they cannot believe that a loving god could allow such things. They cannot separate the existence of an afterlife from the existence of a god. Their incorrect logic is that if a loving god does not exist, then there is no afterlife. However, it is they, themselves, who have allowed such things and they do not recognize this. Often, they do not wish to. They cannot believe that they would be responsible for allowing these bad things into their lives.*

Okay. Another question: When people cross over, we talked about how their beliefs can affect the experience they have. And some people may be disappointed because their belief is not necessarily consistent with what they experience.

*Yes.*

Now, we also talked about how their experience is consistent with their beliefs and this seems confusing.

*At some point the false beliefs will have to crumble like a house of cards. They cannot stand indefinitely.*

But they do stand for a while?

*They will stand as long as you will them to. But there will be spirit guides and other entities who will try to guide you to the reality of the situation. They will do this when they think you are ready.*

So it happens eventually.

*Now this does not mean that you cannot be suddenly shocked that there are no Pearly Gates. This can occur: this type of rude awakening. But often you decide to accept it immediately, you see, and maybe you didn't really believe there were going to be Pearly Gates in the first place, though you professed it over and over in your waking life.*

Right. It depends on the individual because a larger part of that soul-fragment would know they can handle it.

*Yes.*

So initially when people die they pretty much experience what they expect to experience unless they have no expectations?

*Yes.*

But what if some people feel like they absolutely know how it is going to be in their mind and they have very firm beliefs?

*Then they will experience that, at least at first.*

But eventually that will fade away and they will then see the light, so to speak?

*Yes, they will experience a truer awakening to the reality of the situation. Now, reality of course is always subjective and every experience will be slightly different from another and this does not subtract from their truth. However, there is a general basic truth to the way that things run, and Saint Peter at the Pearly Gates is not generally included in this. Any judgment that you face after death is your own. Saint Peter cannot tell you whether you will be admitted to heaven or not. Only you can decide.*

Now, I know there are many different religious ideas about what happens after death such as crossing the River Styx, and some people go straight to hell, and some religions have levels of heaven and some have levels of hell. Those will just be intermediary places, right?

*That is correct and people do experience this very often, just like the bridge or the tunnel. And this happens for as long as the personality must believe it. Many of these religious ideas of heaven are stagnant and if you stay in one place for too long you cannot grow and evolve, and so you must awaken to the larger truth of your own existence and your evolution. So therefore you cannot stay in one place in a heaven or in a hell indefinitely. You will not evolve, you will stagnate, spiritually. This is not the nature of your soul. You must evolve. You must change. It is inevitable.*

Okay. That makes sense. So, what do we get to do after death to evolve?

*That is the next chapter.*

# CHAPTER 8
## SYSTEMS AFTER DEATH

In this chapter Brahma and I discuss the experience a soul has after crossing over. We learn about the importance of balancing the regrets of a life and the ways in which balance can be achieved. Wrongdoings and sins can cause imbalances in the entity but atonement can come in many forms. The soul that lives on has many options of continuing its education and experience through new lives and new realms of existence. Brahma also tells us about the sentiment that a soul retains for those of us that are still living.

---

*Greetings Robert.*

Our next topic is what happens after death.

*Indeed. That is a nice segue from the last conversation.*

Last time we talked about the life review, everything and everyone we've connected with, the feelings and thoughts we would have access to and also being able to know the ways that we, as you said, "have affected the earth" including even things we were unaware of.

*Yes.*

So after we die, do we get answers to all our questions?

*Anything that you can think of that you are curious about you may have an answer to. Now, that answer may require further experience on your part. In other words, you may need to go back to the earthly realm in some sort of memory replay situation to get the answer. Or the answer may be obvious to you, especially if you are asking about other individuals. But you can relive parts of your life and look at them from different perspectives if that is the type of answer that you need or wish for.*

So you can sort of replay situations that you have had in your life with a new perspective in mind and see if it could have turned out differently or to have a better understanding of it?

*Yes, this is correct.*

To learn something else?

*It will not be the same for you as it was when you lived it the first time because your consciousness is not connected to the body consciousness.*

Right. Okay, so sometimes I find myself daydreaming about a movie that I watched the night before and I kind of just replay whole scenes in my head. Is it similar to that? I know it's not the same as watching the movie but I get to replay it somehow.

*An analogy could be drawn in this manner. When one is not incarnate or intimately connected with the body consciousness, there is not the intensity there, but a new perspective can be gained and a peek-in can happen nonetheless. You can relive it, perhaps as though it were a dream or a daydream. You can relive it exactly as it happened in your life or you can change things. You can go back and say, "I wish I had done it this way" and you can do it that way and find out if it is more to your satisfaction.*

So that would be the answer to resolving the regrets that seem to haunt us in our lives: things we wish we hadn't done or the things we wish we had done differently.

*Yes. This is often utilized by personalities who have a heavy mantle of regret as they depart this life and reunite with their entity, or source energy, if you like.*

Right. Speaking of regrets, I would love to think that everything I've done was proper and to not regret anything. We may all have regrets but I was thinking that maybe when we die and try to review a regret, maybe we will figure out that, had we done things differently, we would not have liked the way it would have gone. Maybe the way we actually did it was a very good way of experiencing this world and therefore we should not regret what we have done.

*If you have a regret and you go back and do it a different way and change it, this may satisfy your need to no longer regret the situation. However, some personalities who are dealing with very large regrets may feel a gaping hole in their experience and they will choose to incarnate a new soul-fragment again sooner rather than later to solve the issue.*

Okay.

*Sometimes incarnation is the most immediate way to solve a regret issue. And by immediate I do not mean in terms of time. I mean in terms of intensity.*

Okay, so it may not be enough to just decide to feel better and understand how it would have been better to have acted differently, thereby learning from your mistake. Thinking from the perspective of when you're dead, maybe it would be better to incarnate a new part of your entity to experience a better outcome of a similar situation?

*Yes. Create a freshly minted soul from your entity using the energy of the personality that you are now to create the new soul and then live that way.*

Have them be born into a situation that would likely help with the issue?

*A situation that will help them solve it.*

Solve their regret problem?

*Yes. There are other systems in which one can solve issues and problems, but sometimes when the problem has arisen from an incarnation, it seems to the energy that incarnation is the best or perhaps, only way to solve it. But it depends on the energy. Incarnation is not necessary, but resolution is. Resolution must be reached in some way.*

Okay. But doesn't that make it difficult to incarnate a freshly minted soul to live a similar life and have the same opportunity to make different decisions?

*The life need not be so similar.*

Okay. But how does this newly minted soul keep from making the same mistakes?

*If you were once a slave master and treated your slaves badly, you would not incarnate again necessarily as a slave master. It would be much more to your benefit for resolution to incarnate as a slave. You could resolve it that way. Then you would learn compassion for people who are under your control, you see.*

Okay.

*You can resolve it by playing the other side of the coin. You take the energy that is the slave master and mint from it a slave. And you are not the slave, yet it is part of your energy. So it is not just you, but of you and of your entity. The slave will carry back to you and to the entity its experiences and you, if you are the slave master, will gain compassion from that soul's experience.*

Okay, so in that situation, all that is required is that there be a situation where someone can be born into slavery?

*Yes.*

And the freshly minted soul wouldn't really have to make any difficult decisions and risk making the same mistakes.

*Not necessarily. Now if the entity wanted resolution but wished to cause a further challenge for itself, it would perhaps be a slave master again in a different situation. But this could compound the issue if the soul that is minted does not make the types of decisions that you, the slave master, with regret, has. In which case, more would be needed the next time.*

It could just perpetuate the problem.

*It could. Or it could solve the problem. Most of the time, in situations like this, entities will choose the opposite side of the coin because it is the easiest way, the quickest way, to get the balance back. Achieving balance is very important to the entity.*

Now, it still seems to be a lot of trouble to go through to create balance. Wouldn't it be easier to just peek in on the life of a slave to understand that? I mean, I don't know if the example is part of my confusion, but I can simply just think about being a slave and understand that that is a mistake.

*That is because you have these types of experiences of being under the thumb of someone who is pulling the strings. There are personalities—and in this case the personality we discussed did not have this type of experience—and the only way for this personality to experience such a thing is to be a slave. Looking in would not be enough. Direct experience is needed in this case. You, Robert, can just think of such a thing because you have been in such a position before.*

When the slave master personality with all the regrets died and crossed over, wouldn't they have access to the perspective they didn't have?

*They would have access to some perspective but it would be sort of an outsider's perspective, and there would more than likely be a desire within the personality to more fully experience that which was dealt out.*

So it stems from the desire to experience it?

*Yes, there is a desire for balance, and if you are the slave master and you die and you have access to the feelings of those you treated wrongly, it will more than likely spark a desire in you to know more about these feelings that you have caused.*

It is not because they want to punish themselves?

*It is not punishment, no. It is the desire for balance. It is the desire to truly understand the other side of an equation.*

Right, but it seems as though the equation has already been solved and that is the reason for the regret.

*It has not been solved. It has been opened for inspection. It has been cracked as an acorn and now the acorn can be seen. There is a desire to inspect the acorn, to investigate the feeling of regret. But now that it is known that there is an acorn, there is a desire to know more about this acorn of regret. It must be explored and understood, and balance must be achieved.*

So it's more about direct individual experience within an entity family, and not being able to benefit from the experience of another entity?

*That is correct.*

Because surely there would be a slave somewhere who you might talk to after you are both dead?

*Yes, of course. And you will have access to some of the feelings that you caused.*

And you might ask how it was?

*Yes, but you will then desire to know more about what it was like for the other side.*

So it is just purely a desire for fully direct experience?

*Yes, full direct understanding. It is knowledge in its purest, finest form.*

It is not the case that this soul is just so thick-headed that they just don't get it? It seems obvious to me that I do not want to be a slave and that one slave is too many slaves.

*But you have experienced being a slave before, so you know that it is not something that you wish to experience again.*

I have experience being a slave?

*Yes. It is a common part of a complete soul experience. Many of you have had this type of experience.*

So you are saying that my perspective is biased?

*You understand it, so you do not need to go in that direction. You also are not that type of person, because you have the understanding of a previous life involving slavery. You have the compassion not to put those who could be considered to be beneath you under your thumb in such a severe manner because you know what it feels like. It has created some compassion in you for your fellow humans and for fellow animals as well.*

But not every soul has the benefit of that perspective?

*That is correct.*

So there is a reason why it seems so obvious to me?

*Yes, because you, your greater entity family, have had direct experience. Not everyone has this. Bronwen too, has direct experience of course. Many of you with a fair amount of general compassion have direct experience. It is the thick-headed numbskulls that go around stepping on everyone that have not had this experience.*

Aha! So there actually are thick-headed numbskull souls?

*Naturally, of course. But they will learn. Enlightenment is their destiny, and it is their destiny to be a slave if they are treating others as such. They will desire it. They will need it.*

So they can just go be each other's slaves?

*Yes, of course.*

Is there any way they can do it somewhere else? I do not want to see it or be a part of it.

*You do not have to be involved in this, Robert. We understand. You are past that. It is not necessary for you.*

---

Okay, so most of the time it seems like we freshly minted souls live our lives and make our own decisions. If there is something that our larger entity would like to resolve or even would like us to experience or learn, why does it seem like they are so detached? Why does it seem that they have a hands-off approach? Is that required? Why wouldn't the entity be more involved in the life of the freshly minted soul in helping them have a certain experience?

*Each soul-fragment is granted complete free will. Without complete free will the education is not as complete. You cannot learn as well as you can through experience and your experience must be that of your own choosing in order to experience it fully. In order to be Mother Teresa you must be able to choose to be Saddam Hussein, in order to have it mean anything.*

Right.

*If you are forced or gently led like a child in a certain direction, the balance will not be achieved. It must be chosen freely.*

That makes sense. What if the newly minted soul asks for help?

*The entity will do its best to communicate with the soul. The soul must be open to receiving help, must listen, must hear, must feel and intuit for the guidance of the entity. Many times you close yourselves off to this. The entity is always happy to be of assistance but the entity must be listened to and be heard in order for help to arrive. There are other guides as well which the entity is in communication with. These guides can sometimes help you when the entity cannot be heard. Sometimes.*

So these guides, and the entity, are the ones listening to our prayers and are effectively what we are praying to when we are asking for help by praying?

*Essentially. This is it.*

They are the gods. Or The God. Correct?

*However, gods can be created by human minds. They will not be as powerful as entity energy in most cases. But they can gain power from human thought.*

Okay.

*They are creations of thought, just like you are. But because they are from the earthly realm of newly minted souls and earthly thoughts, they may not be as powerful as you.*

That could be quite disappointing for some to find out when they die.

*It could indeed. But these figures are more important for you when you are on Earth if you believe in them. Many times when one crosses over, these phantoms are quickly dissipated because they are no longer needed, at least for the personality involved. By dissipated I do not mean that they disappear. I mean that they become less important and this is seen. This is recognized.*

So, getting back to the reliving of our experiences, you mentioned we could tap into the worldview of others in the last chapter. For example, we could be able to have an understanding of what it was like for Socrates to live his life. Is there some kind of library of lives where we can check out a book on someone's life and read their story?

*Experiencing the worldview of someone else could be thought of as reading a book perhaps if the story was written in the first person. It would be a little like stepping into their shoes for a moment, like being an actor playing that character for a moment. You would know the things that you would say if you were that person and the things that you would think in a given situation. The experience gives you their worldview.*

So you would play the role of their character?

*In a sense, yes.*

And have their experience?

*You would understand that it was not you. It may or may not be their experience. It will be their perspective though.*

Right. Now, in thinking about this, that can be very helpful in understanding other points of view, other perspectives of life.

*It is indeed very helpful.*

It could even be very inspiring to say, "Gosh, I really enjoyed that person's life". Couldn't that inspire you to create a new soul-fragment and throw it into a similar situation to have a similar experience?

*Of course, if you are so inspired, you can do that. You would have to take from the resources that you have available, but inspiration could create something or someone new from this. Again you must use your own resources, those of your entity. If you have no lavender you cannot throw it into the mix, so to speak.*

It's easy to imagine reading a book sometimes and thinking to myself, even if the book is written in first person, "Oh I wouldn't have done that. I would've done something different." But the story could be compelling enough that I would like to play that role.

*Yes, you may certainly do that.*

And probably do things differently.

*Although, it will not be you in a sense. It will be of you, so you will be more of a watcher. However you can live vicariously if you choose. You can step into them for moments.*

Okay. So does that imply that after I die, I can create new souls to go out and have experiences and I can live vicariously through them? But do I have to wait until they die before I get all of their experience?

*No. It is ongoing.*

It is ongoing. It is always live?

*Yes.*

So everything that I am doing here now, my entity has a constant streaming feed of my experience?

*Yes, this is correct. You have a wonderful understanding.*

So I am always being watched?

*In a sense you are. The entity can choose to pay attention to something else. But yes, you are always part of it. It is always aware of you.*

I guess that's part of my next question. We live in a part of reality here where deception is a common part of our lives. We like keeping to ourselves and not revealing everything to each other. We enjoy being alone and having our private thoughts, our privacy, I suppose. I know there are no secrets after death, but while we are living...

*And you are asking me if your life is not truly private?*

Yes. That is my question.

*No, it is not.*

My life is not private?

*However, your entity does not judge you in a way that you judge or feel you are being judged by others in this reality. Your entity has only loving energy for you and wishes you well.*

No matter what I do?

*Yes. No matter what you do. That is correct. Although, your entity might see something and think, "Ooh, we're going to need to fix that next time." Perhaps. It might try to communicate with you in order to help you fix it this time, if it seems fixable or if it seems that you are willing or wish to do so.*

Okay. So, are there truly things that we should not do, then? Are there things that we might want to fix? Specifically, are there wrong decisions and wrong actions that we take?

*Yes. Taking the life of another is a wrong action, for example. Now, this does not apply to lions in the savanna taking down a gazelle. But, it applies to needless taking of life.*

So it is situational?

*Yes. But most of you know when this is wrong and when this is not. The entity knows. It is against moral law in the planes that we come from.*

So, if there is a moral law, then there are sins?

*Yes, but you will not go to Hell for them.*

Right. But, I mean actions that are inherently wrong, things that we should not do.

*Yes, that is correct. There are things that you should not do. Not that the consequences will be as many imagine them. There is no devil. There is no hell. There can be great sadness and disappointment in our realms. It causes disruption. It is disruptive, and the taking of another's earthly life before they are finished is not, shall we say, proper.*

Now, when someone dies and this person has committed one of these deeds like killing someone prematurely, do they get to work this out?

*Yes. They must.*

Okay. Now, in the case of a deed that was done that did not involve killing and was just a case where one person wronged another, can this be resolved between the two parties and therefore make it not a sin with the sinful complications? Does it depend upon the parties involved and their thoughts and feelings about the actions, whether or not it is a sin?

*Yes.*

So if one dead person says to another, "You wronged me, but I forgive you and you understand why you did that and why it was wrong." Then can they effectively...

*...wipe the slate clean?*

Yes.

*Yes. They can do this if they both agree.*

Okay.

*Or, they can resolve the issue in another incarnation.*

So there is forgiveness?

*Yes. But if it does involve another individual, both individuals must agree that the slate is balanced and clean.*

That seems like that's the most important aspect of any wrongdoing.

*Yes, but some resolution must come. If one takes a life against our moral law, then it must be atoned for in some way. Some resolution must come to the energy that has been wronged. Now, this does not apply to Kevorkian-type cases of assisted suicide, of course.*

Right, because the person being killed wants to die.

*Yes. That is different if they are choosing to go. It is not a sin. It is only in the case of taking of life against the wishes of that life that there is a wrongdoing.*

Are there other situations in which the life being taken wants to be taken but the consciousness or the ego of that person doesn't know it? And they therefore fight for their life even though, spiritually, they really want to die?

*This can happen. In some cases this happens in an atonement issue.*

Where they signed up to be killed in a certain way to balance the entity?

*It is wrong but it re-balances. It is difficult to explain because when you have a law in your reality there are consequences for breaking it. And there are consequences in our reality too, but they are not penal consequences, you see.*

Right.

*So it is difficult to explain in your terms.*

Right. It is just a balancing of an equation.

*Yes, and killing against the will of an energy seems to be the most unbalancing and disruptive. Also, this is because the energy of this proposed person had plans to balance many things in a life perhaps, and the life was cut short.*

Right. So now they have to start over again?

*Yes. With a newly minted soul. They cannot do it themselves, they must send a messenger.*

Right. It has to be a new soul-fragment through which they can experience the balancing vicariously.

*It can be frustrating.*

So, thinking about all of the terrible wars that we have had here, there must be a lot of people up there with unfinished lives.

*There are many unfinished lives, yes.*

Now, do these wars perpetuate because of these unfinished lives?

*In some cases they do.*

Do the killers have to go back and be killed?

*That is not necessary. Sometimes the parties agree that this is the only way to resolve the issue. It is not necessary though. For example, in the book, <u>Messages From Michael</u> [9] was a situation where a man killed another man and the victim returned in another life as a surgeon and performed an operation on the man who had killed him. Just physically cutting him was enough to re-balance and resolve the issue between the two entities. Although he was doing the man service by operating on him, he did cut the flesh which had an effect that was enough for both parties.*

Okay. I like that better then. I'd hate to think that somebody would have to go to war again and be the one killed.

*No. There are what you may think of as karmic consequences for killing. So, many times those killed do not wish to do that. When one kills, it attaches energies to the entity that are not easily dispelled. So, if it is a re-balancing, and you are the victim, you may choose something different for your own preservation of disrupted energy.*

Okay. All so very complicated: all of this balancing of different experiences. When I die, am I going to be able to know all of these unbalances and re-balances and all these wonderful stories about entities re-balancing?

*If you wish to, you may tap into them. It is up to you.*

Is there a way for me to know this information here while I'm alive? Through my entities, perhaps? Only if I ask, maybe?

*Which information are you speaking of?*

Okay. My question is: does my life have any re-balancing to do? I assume I have to experience everything without coaching, but I guess I would like to know what my purpose here is. Or at least one of my purposes?

*For you, Robert, your purpose has been to learn compassion. It is always to gain understanding for everyone, but in your case in particular, it is to gain compassion. In this regard, you have speedily raced upon that track. You have done everything and more that your entity wished you to do in that department. However, there are other reasons you are here. Some of them are of your own devising. You are here to*

---

[9] **by Chelsea Quinn Yarbro, 2005**

*encourage technology. Your thoughts and feelings and fascination with this area of reality helps with the discovery and creation of new technology. You are to go as far as you can in this area, as far as is interesting to you. You are also here to help the animals that you help. You are here to lead people in directions that are beneficial to them.*

Is it important that these types of re-balancing are not known to me or to the life of people with similar situations in order to achieve them?

*If you do not consciously know them, you intuitively understand some of them.*

I was thinking that my path towards compassionate living would not have been the same had I not figured it out for myself. Would I have been the same if somebody had said, "You should be more compassionate"?

*No, it does not work this way; it must come from you. Otherwise, it is of no use to the entity.*

So, I imagine for most of us then, we don't know our purposes until we've achieved them.

*Many times this is true, although you come up with new purposes throughout your lifetime and your entity may see some potential in you and give you another idea that you can choose to follow or not of your own free will.*

I really love that. Free will.

*Yes. It is granted to all creations.*

Okay. Now to stay on track here, I have more questions about the systems you spoke of.

*Very good.*

So, what else is there to do after you die?

*That is a very general question.*

Okay. We can relive our lives and replay our memories and tap into the lives of others, correct?

*You can look in on the lives of others that you knew when you were alive that are still living if you like. You can reunite with those who knew you in your lifetime. There are other realities that you can choose to participate in that are not earthly incarnations. There are other types of incarnations in realities that have different intensities and different rules. There are different types of incarnations where you may choose to have experiences like your earthly ones, which you may choose to do without focusing on an earthly incarnation. It is likely that you will wind up doing some of these other things in any case since going back to Earth can only be done vicariously. A new soul-fragment sent to an earthly experience cannot be you directly, although the new incarnation is a soul-fragment that is* of *you.*

Right. So do you mean we can experience realities like other planets?

*If you prefer. Or other realities entirely. There are some that are similar to Earth but have different rules. There are realities where gravity is different, for instance. One can fly if one chooses. They have different laws.*

Like laws of physics?

*Yes, in different planes of experience. Some of these you have experienced in your dream states. Some of them are actual realities that you go to and some are of your own making that you go to in your dreams. But there are systems that you go to that are actual systems that you can choose to go to and experience after you cross over.*

Do you mean systems like this reality here which seems to be a very complex system?

*Yes. There are similar systems and even more complex ones. This one, your earthly reality, has a particular intensity that draws courageous souls. One must have some degree of courage to come here.*

Courage? Is this reality that bad?

*You are amusing, my friend! (Laughing) But yes, in a sense. It is intense.*

I imagine it's like opting to play a difficult and challenging game.

*Yes, as opposed to one that is easier and perhaps more suited to your level. Although, there are some of you that are of a very suitable level for your reality.*

Right, you don't want to play a boring game necessarily if you think you might have the courage and skill to master a more difficult one.

*Yes, indeed.*

And of course, usually playing a very difficult game has the potential to be very rewarding. Is that true in this case?

*Yes. Absolutely.*

Or maybe just very frustrating.

*It can be both. It is thought of as a very challenging system. There are systems that are easier and perhaps more fun. But then you do not have the same challenge, as you pointed out. You can choose to briefly visit these systems or choose to have a whole incarnation in one of them. You can choose to create your own realities and systems if you have the talent and inclination. You can step into the worldview of others. You can have an advanced education if you wish.*

*There are systems you can go to where you can retain the personality that you have now without an incarnation and simply learn. This is sort of like taking classes. But not exactly the same. But there are teachers there who will help you learn things without experiencing them. Then you may wish to take this experience to another system to try it out.*

So like a training class?

*Yes, in a sense. There are teachers in many areas who wish to simply teach and help any who wish to gather around them. Their desire is to teach what they know for the benefit of all, you see. You can also become one of these teachers if you have the aptitude and you would like to.*

To teach what I know about, for example, this reality?

*Yes, if you prefer, you certainly could. If there were those entities who were unsure about coming here, they might come to you if you were holding an open class, for example. You might advertise: "Any who wish to learn about this particular aspect of this reality, come to me." From this exchange, they could decide whether or not they wished to have the experience for themselves. Or, if they have already decided to incarnate for the experience, they could get information from you that would make it easier to navigate on this plane.*

*This is kind of like having skiing lessons first or just pushing yourself down the hill for the first time. Sometimes you are fine going down the hill with no idea what you should be doing, learning as you go. Sometimes it would be better to have a lesson first. There are also those who can teach you how to build other realities and there are classes, if you will, that you could go to. You do not sit in a little room with a desk however, you see. It is a gathering and it is in a place where all of these energies wish to be.*

So is that why some people are more successful in life? Maybe they brushed up on earthly moneymaking or something.

*In some cases, it is. Sometimes they simply have excellent resources from their entity to draw upon and they have an open channel to this resource. That can be another reason why they are successful. But yes, sometimes they have had the benefit of teachers before arriving.*

So if somebody has taken a class in earthly living and their entity is quite experienced in earth, they could come here and be like a superhero? Or at least, very successful?

*Yes, if they wish. Although, success in our realm is not measured by money or power necessarily.*

Right.

*Success is the progression of the life and the answering of the question of whether it did what it was meant to do. Did it find some new purpose to progress along those lines that the entity hadn't even thought of. There are many measures and determinations of success that are not necessarily the same as they are here.*

Right. I was thinking of success as being a life of discovery and learning without the frustration and sadness and things that we think of as negative experiences here.

*Yes, that would certainly be one definition of success. That would be a very good way to live, to learn, if you could learn without this sadness and frustration. Although, some cannot do this as there are many lessons to be learned from mistakes and frustrations.*

Okay. So, when you die you get to go share experiences with your larger entity and with other entities. Do you sit around and exchange stories? Is that fun?

*If you would like to, you may do that.*

Because that seems like it would be fun. To sit around in big comfy chairs and exchange life stories.

*If that is your wish, you may do that. It certainly happens.*

Is it easier to convey your stories after you die? It seems like you might have better methods of communication than we have here.

*Yes. Everyone is an open book. There are no secrets, no lies. It is very easy.*

So you don't even have to talk?

*No, speaking is not necessary. You may speak if you wish. There is somewhat of a universal language that is not English. It is understood by all.*

It is telepathic?

*Yes, but you may speak the words if you wish to add inflection or attach sounds to your stories.*

Right.

Now, when I die am I going to be able to remember things that I cannot seem to remember now?

*You can recall anything you wish to recall.*

Because I know there are things that I have completely forgotten about.

*If you wish to recall them they will be available to you.*

Now? Or only after I die?

*When you die all will be available to you. It will be available to you now if you have the ability to recall it. You can ask for assistance from your entity or your guides if you wish to recall something that you cannot. They may be able to help you.*

But some of that depends upon my awareness at the time that I experienced it and whether or not I was really paying attention. Right?

*Perhaps.*

I was just thinking that experiences are usually easier, but say I read a textbook for a class and then I fail a test because I never really actually learned the material. Or was it the case that I did learn it but then I later forgot it?

*You read it but if you didn't think about it when you read it, the meaning will be lost on you anyway. You have to comprehend it. Now, if you read it, you could perhaps recall the words, but you would not recall the comprehension if it was never there.*

Because I never actually did learn it?

*Yes.*

---

So is there a giant hard drive in the sky that is recording all of my experiences?

*In a sense.*

That I will have access to when I die?

*Yes, in a sense. There is something similar to recordings that you will have access to in recalling your experiences.*

Will I remember the names of people I cannot remember now?

*Yes, absolutely.*

That is good to know because we tend to think of memory as being a construct of the brain, and experience as having more to do with the soul.

*Everything is recorded. You will have access to everything that was recorded as far as that goes.*

That's cool.

*There are different ways one can access these recordings or records. They have also been referred to as the Akashic records. You may read them. You may view them as in a movie. You may re-experience them. There are many ways to access these once you have crossed over. It is very individual to the personality which way is most comfortable or desirable.*

So it is like a library?

*In a sense. But with different ways of viewing the same information.*

Like different forms of media?

*Yes. You may wish to hear it or see it or read about it, for example.*

Right, movies or books or fully immersive rooms of virtual realities?

*Yes.*

Like the ultimate library.

*Yes. Many of you spend much time doing these sorts of things after you first crossover because it seems so interesting.*

Well, yeah, I bet it would be. I imagine I'll have even more questions about my life after I die.

*Yes. You will have a much greater understanding of your life because you will be in a different frame of mind, so to speak, looking from a different perspective.*

So everything I've ever wondered about I can find the answers to?

*Yes, although the answers may need to come in the form of an incarnation if it is the answer to an unresolved issue, for instance.*

So some questions may be too complex to answer by simply reading about them?

*Yes.*

But for every fascination I've had, I can get an answer?

*Yes, you may have to create an incarnation of a dragonfly to know what its existence is like, for example, unless your entity has already done such a thing, and then you would have access to it.*

But if I just had a mild fascination of what it's like to be a dragonfly, then I could get a general idea.

*Well, you must have experience as a dragonfly to really know the answer to the question of what it is like to be a dragonfly. Your entity must already have an experience or you must create one. But if your entity already has an experience of a dragonfly in some incarnation, you will have access to that, you see.*

Does the information have to be within my own entity's experience?

*It is possible to tap into the world view of a dragonfly that is not of your entity. However, this is not the usual method.*

Right. Why would you when you could just become one yourself? It's not like you don't have time.

*Yes. The entity creates experience. It is the thing it most craves. So if you really, really wonder, it would be best for the entity to just give it a try.*

Right, because experience is better than knowledge?

*Yes and the world view of a dragonfly might be somewhat disappointing, whereas the experience of flying around could be exhilarating.*

Right, because that could be the best part about being a dragonfly.

*Yes, indeed.*

So after people get tired of spending all this time experiencing or reliving or learning all this stuff that they wondered about, then what else? They then go on to create realities and become teachers?

*Yes, they become teachers, they create other worlds, and more. There are endless fascinations, endless diversions. If one wishes to, it is possible to reunite with the energy of the entity. One may do that for a while and become more of a 'we' than an 'I', in a sense. The soul-fragment still has free will, so if it wishes to retain more of an independence from the entity it may. But if it chooses to have more access to other aspects of the entity it can merge with it and actually become the 'we', you see.*

So even after you die, your soul continues on, evolves, and acquires more experience?

*Yes.*

I assume there are experiences that we would have trouble understanding. Right?

*Yes, one can acquire experience in ways that you can understand, but also in ways that you probably wouldn't even consider.*

You have mentioned in the chapter on the death experience that we have a detached compassion when we die. Does that mean we don't worry about what's going on here but we still care?

*Yes. That is a correct assessment.*

So is that why those of us that survive feel like we are being a little abandoned?

*Yes, perhaps that is part of it.*

They still care but they don't worry anymore and that kind of makes us feel left behind?

*Yes. One may not understand that one can care and not worry, perhaps.*

But they do care? Right?

*Yes. They care deeply.*

I guess that's what I wanted to hear. It's what we all want to hear from our departed love ones.

*Of course, love continues. It does not go away.*

Knowing that there is so much wonderful stuff to do after death, it seems as though when someone dies they might just forget about us.

*At times they do, but not forever. For moments perhaps they turn their attention away but they always will be with you, connected by the love energy as well. And if you think of them they will be available.*

Do I have to think of them with the love energy?

*Not necessarily. What do you mean by this?*

If I think of somebody that died, in a not so loving way, would they still be available? Or do I have to think of them lovingly?

*It has to be an energy connection of some kind. Some sort of emotion must be attached. Love is just the strongest emotion.*

Okay. Another question regarding departed souls: From our perspective, we are here and all you other nonphysical beings are there somewhere in the afterlife. I am assuming that your perspective is similar to that of those who have died. You mentioned that there are different energies of dead people that are closer to your energy, and we talked about how some energies are foreign to you, and you said you do not have much to say in enticing them to conversation.

*Yes.*

You have a close connection with Bronwen that allows her to channel you, but it appears that you do not have much conversation with other entities directly.

*You are accusing me of not socializing with other entities?*

Well, no. I guess I'm wondering why Bronwen can channel you, Brahma, but not some random person's dead grandmother.

*Well, if the dead grandmother in question happened to be from the Brahma group of souls, then perhaps it would be possible.*

Right, I think I understand that. But I also thought that we were all connected somehow and that everyone is supposedly spiritually connected to everyone else.

*Think of it this way: Your eyes are in your body and your mouth is on your body. So are your toes, but your eyes and your mouth communicate with each other a lot better than your eyes and your toes. You can feel the pull on your eyes when you speak. When you smile you can feel the crinkle in your eyes from your mouth, but you do not feel much in your toes. You see, these are parts of the same being but some are further removed from other parts.*

Okay.

*You cannot as easily feel something that your toe does with your eyes as you can feel something that your mouth does with your eyes. Do you understand?*

Yes. That makes sense to me. So then what about certain medium psychics who seem to be able to relay messages from people who have crossed over to people who are still living here?

*There are those among you who are open conduits and they can speak with many different types of energies because they are so open.*

Is it because they are open or because they are just really popular among dead people?

*(Laughing) They are open and therefore they are popular. Because of their openness they draw to them many different types of energies that wish to express themselves through the conduit.*

Okay.

*Not everyone can do this.*

Right.

*It is a special gift.*

And is this so different from channeling?

*It is a similar type of action. It is a similar way of doing things, but it is not the same as what we are doing now.*

Okay.

*Bronwen does not have this open conduit ability. She does not speak to everyone.*

Can you talk to these other spirits?

*It depends upon their energy. If the energy is similar enough to mine I can speak to them. If it is too different it would be difficult.*

So all these people that have crossed over, they don't necessarily get to talk to each other?

*If there is a strong emotional pull between them they will.*

Do you mean like if they knew each other when they were alive?

*Yes.*

I'm trying to understand the situation where I've seen psychics or mediums who are conveying messages to a group of people, and they are getting messages from beyond. It seems like spirits are all just hanging around the psychic. Is it possible that they actually might not even be aware of each other?

*Yes, they might not be aware of each other. This is correct. And sometimes the psychics will feel spirits fighting to talk to them because they are unaware of each other. But they are all aware of the psychic.*

Like a phone call where were they don't know someone else is calling at the same time.

*Yes.*

It seems that there is a commonly held belief that once people die, they all go to the afterlife and will run into each other whether they knew each other in life or not.

*This is not the case. There must be some sort of desire for the most part. However, an accidental meeting can occur if the right time and space and intention are the focus of the soul-fragments.*

So, for example if somebody crosses over who knew two different people who didn't know each other, when they all three crossover they might be able to know each other through the common friend?

*Yes, of course. If they were both focusing on the same person or situation or idea, they may sense each other and become acquainted that way. They may also learn of the others' existence when researching worldviews for example and spark a desire to know each other. It's important to remember that in any case, there will not be a feeling of being among strangers like you have experienced in your physical incarnation.*

Okay.

It just occurred to me because we talked about all the things that you can do after death and the types of experience one could have, most of them being a vicarious experience. But it seems like, to a degree, everything is vicarious. Because if I wanted to experience being a slave I would have to create a new soul and that soul would have firsthand experience. It wouldn't necessarily be me.

*This is correct, however it can be a more intense vicarious experience if you allow it to be.*

So there are different degrees of vicariousness?

*Yes, and something that you create directly for the purposes of your own experience can be more intense than looking over your best friend's shoulder, for example.*

Okay. So that is what I suspected. There are different levels of vicarious experience.

*Yes, and it is up to you how strongly you experience these things. You could for instance, feel like: "Well I need a little bit of a slave experience, but not much, so I'll create a slave personality but I only look in now and then or a little bit."*

Okay.

*Or you can place yourself within this slave personality and experience every breath if you chose. You will desire what is necessary for yourself, for your evolution and growth and enlightenment.*

Okay.

*As I have said, most of you have compassion in this life, and most of our readers will have already experienced being in this slave type of position and will have no further use of it or need for it. So do not worry about the unpleasantries of being a slave.*

# CHAPTER 9
## ATTACHMENTS IN THE PHYSICAL AND BEYOND

Even after they pass on to the afterlife, souls have lingering spiritual attachments to people and places. In this continuing discussion on death and beyond, we learn about the relationships of souls. These relationships may be formed before a person is born into physical life or made at some point during their lives.

*Greetings from beyond.*

Hello, Brahma. Can I ask about spiritual attachments?

*I will do my best.*

All of us at some point in our lives have relationships with others or attachments of some sort. Do they continue beyond death?

*Those on this plane are very concerned about the relationships they develop here or the relationships that were present before they arrived. Many of you believe that death or moving away from a land is the end of a relationship. However, most often this is not the case.*

So when somebody crosses over in the death experience is it the same as just moving to a new city? You can still maintain relationships even though you are no longer present?

*It is similar to moving to a new city.*

But do we just leave everything behind in the old city and continue on? Or are we more sentimental? Do we invite those old friends to come hang out with us in the afterlife when they crossover?

*If it is desired, you may continue your relationship in a similar vein when you both have crossed over. However, if it is a close relationship, it still continues when one is still in the physical realm and the other is not. Communication takes place in the dream state and through consciousness lapses throughout the day, and if one pays attention, one can pinpoint communications from the other while they are conscious as well. Many of these relationships began way before their physical life. There are entities and entity groups, or groups of souls if you will, that have attachments to each other, strong attachments, intimate relationships. There are souls and groups of souls which wish to incarnate together again and again. This is not only because there is a love or a friendship between them but also because it has proven to be beneficial for learning throughout millennia or through many different experiences of incarnations of this type as well as other types.*

So it's beneficial for learning? Is that because they, in a manner of speaking, share a common background?

*This can be the case. There are different types of relationships that are beneficial for learning. Some of them are cooperative relationships where the incarnations of the souls get along very well and share a common goal. Some of these are adversarial relationships where learning takes place in the overcoming of an adversity. Some will incarnate again and again with those that they cannot stand or with those that just rub them the wrong way. This is an eternal search, for lack of a better word, to find peace and common ground within the adversity.*

So does that indicate that there is sort of a conflict that wants to work itself out?

*Yes. This is sometimes the case and may require many sorts of relationships and incarnations. But you see, the universe, as you have been instructed, does not hear, "Not...", "I hate...", "I do not want...". It does not avoid things that are focused on. If an energy is visible in your mind, you are attracting that energy whether it is the adverse parts of it you're thinking about or a loving part. So an energy can be attracted to another energy it cannot stand and incarnate again and again to resolve the issue. Once the issue is resolved the soul may discover it has nothing more in common with this energy and will forget about it and move on. Or perhaps it will discover it has a lot in common with this energy. That perhaps is the reason for the adversity and perhaps they will then develop a more loving relationship.*

Okay. So, there are people in our lives, or for example from my point of view, that I am in contact with, living with, having this life experience with, that I have some connection with from before we were born?

*Yes.*

Now, I don't know exactly how this works, but I do know that sometimes it's hard for us to connect with old friends when we both live in the same town. Isn't it difficult for people to coordinate with their different experiences and different lives and the experiences they are trying to have and still be able to reconnect with people or souls or entities that they are already acquainted with from before birth?

*Are you speaking about this life or beyond?*

In this life. Say I have a friend, or actually, say that the souls of my entity have ongoing relationships with other souls, and one of those incarnates lives here in the same town as I do. Do I necessarily reconnect with this person? Wouldn't it be difficult to get together with this old friend with a stranger's face?

*If there is an agreement to connect and a reason to do so, there will be a point of attraction which enables a meeting. The energies will be drawn together. There is no need to worry about that.*

So it would be through some attraction because we have a similar interest or something like that?

*Or there is an attraction from energy to energy. Your friend's energy and your energy will be attracted to each other based on a previous set meeting or on a need to meet in this incarnation now.*

And that would be a point of attraction?

*Yes, the energies will be drawn together to connect when it is beneficial and sometimes agreed upon.*

Okay. Now, when people connect here on Earth either for the first time or for a re-acquaintance, do they get to hang out together in the afterlife?

*If you have had a true relationship and a true love for each other, you can hang out with your friends as much as you prefer. Some of these friends will have similar goals to you and you may want to 'take a class' together, in a sense. You may want to gather your energies and learn from other energies in the same environment or you may want to teach together if there is something to teach that you are both familiar with. There are many things you can do together.*

*You can also create another incarnation in another reality or you can create realities together. These can be sort of dream realities from thin air and you can design them how you wish and have fun and create your own little private nest, if you will, that is accessible only to you unless you invite someone else in. There is opportunity for privacy if you wish or you may be together in more public forums or you may go your separate ways and occasionally meet up to compare notes, as you desire.*

This sounds like you can catch up with old friends and loved ones. Correct?

*Yes, you may wish to continue the relationship you had or you may wish to just say hello, go your separate ways, and perhaps reconnect at a later point. It is based on the desires of both parties. There is not usually, as some people believe, an eternal soul mate. There are sometimes energies that do not appear to leave each other's sides, but this is the closest that comes to soulmates. But even with these close energies there is no eternal promise of "until forever do us part". The energies just continue to like to hang out together and so they continue to do so. There is no law that says they must or they must not cheat on each other or any such thing like this.*

So there are really just highly compatible personalities. There are not two halves of a soul that are going to reconnect after death to become a whole soul. Right?

*Well in a way, you are all fragments of a whole soul or entity. But then you would have many, many, many soulmates within your soul entity and eventually if you trace it to the top of the pyramid or family tree you will be soul mates with everyone.*

So there aren't just two souls in a soulmate?

*Correct. Although two can stay together and experience time, so to speak, together for many millennia in your terms, if they wish. There's no law against it, but there is no binding spiritual tie that controls their destiny.*

Okay.

*It must continue to be mutually wanted and beneficial for both parties.*

Right.

## Attachments in the Physical and Beyond

Now, as far as attachments in the physical world, I know many people are afraid of losing what they have here and that contributes to a fear of death. Among the things that they fear are being alone or being away from loved ones. But that is not really the case, is it?

*Those who feel alone are generally those who remain here. Most of the time when you cross over you will meet so many friends it is almost impossible to feel alone, and in your terms, at that time your loved one who survived you will be right behind you. There will not be a terribly long time for you to miss them. However from the point of view of the living, you might seem to be apart for a very long time.*

Is that because you don't experience time in the same way after you cross over?

*That is correct and you will generally have very much to do, will be very engaged, and will have very many other relationships to occupy you in the meantime. If a living person was important to you, you will of course be there when they crossover. You will know exactly when this happens. You will not miss your appointment if you wish to have one.*

So regarding the separation of death, you might say that the only tortured souls are the ones that stay behind. Correct?

*That is generally the case. Now, you can torture yourself if you are in the other realm if you are not accepting of your current reality. If you do not believe that you deserve to have a good time, if you believe that you are deserving of hell or suffering, you may create this for yourself as I have mentioned in the chapter on the death experience. But if you are accepting of the true reality, then you will meet with friends and you'll come home to your entity and you will feel loved, supported, and fulfilled. If you do not and you refuse to see this and you instead see yourself in a prison cell, there are spiritual guides who will try to guide you out of it and towards the true reality. Eventually you will get there. Hopefully, you will get there right away. It would be more pleasant for you. I do not anticipate that you, Robert, will have very much trouble with this.*

I don't either. I think I'm lucky. I don't feel like I have many fears of death.

*That is intelligent and enviable for some.*

Now, this chapter is about attachments to the physical world and apparently there are attachments with other personalities and souls that transfer after death. Are there physical attachments, like places attachments? Are there places or locations that people get attached to?

*There are places on the earthly plane that those who are not currently incarnated in the physical will re-create because they are so attached to them. There will be another version of it in your realm if you wish there to be. If you are so attached to a place that you think of it often and wish to be there, you can create another version that you can go to at any time. You may visit the one on Earth as well but that is not as easy for you to do. It takes a different focus of energy to come to this earthly plane. When you are there it is more challenging to maintain the focus, though it can be done. But there generally does not seem to be a need for this since you can create not only your little paradise that you love but you can create it in ways that are better than the original.*

So if you have a particular place you like to go to, maybe it's a park with a pond and a tree, you can create a duplicate in some sort of sandbox reality or other realms that are not earthly realms?

*Yes. The one on Earth may, for instance, have mosquitoes. You can create this without mosquitoes, you see.*

Awesome. But I can still have frogs, right?

*Indeed. You can add little touches of perfection to make it even more enjoyable.*

And that would be favorable to spawning a new soul that could come to Earth and live and hang out in that area?

*Though you may want to do this in any case.*

But that can be sort of a vicarious experience. Is creating your own park a more direct experience?

*Yes. It is more vicarious to experience it through a newly minted soul. Your created park affords a more interactive experience.*

Even though it's more intensely focused for the living soul, the soul in the afterlife may still wish to create their own park.

*Yes. The soul that you create and send back to your pond is sort of like having an IV drip: you will get the benefits of it, but it is not the same as the genuine experience. You are still experiencing the pond in a sense. It is contributing to your life, but you are also experiencing things elsewhere.*

Right. It is like a simulation, because it's almost like a secondhand experience?

*Yes. You can of course step into their shoes for periods of time if you like, which is more of a firsthand experience, but you will not be the guiding decider.*

No. And the living souls have to be open to this stepping in?

*Yes. Well, generally they are a part of you and they do not have a problem with this, and most of the time they do not even realize it. But still, they must make their own decisions. You can nudge them if you like. But it must be their choice to walk over to the bench and sit by the pond or sit on the grass under a tree.*

---

Now, I have a question about the things that we enjoy here and the things we enjoy after we cross over. It's my understanding that our knowledge and experience comes with us when we cross over. Does everything come with us? For example, does our intellect come with us? It seems I use my brain to do math, for instance, and when I am dreaming, I have trouble doing math. In this case I seem to be leaving part of my analyzing abilities in my brain.

*That is correct.*

My brain is a tool that helps me do calculations in my head. Do I get to bring this with me?

*You do not bring your brain.*

Of course. I know. That would be weird.

*You have an energy intelligence which you bring and your mind which you bring. Math is not necessary to calculate in the other realms. It is automatically calculated if needed. It is not necessary to work it out in a long division problem like you do here.*

Okay. So we don't need these tools like brains. Is that the same for other skills that we have practiced and learned here in our physical life?

*If you wish to play piano, you can play piano. But it will not be the same tactile experience as it is in the physical life.*

I ask because some of us here are really good at physical things. Some have worked many years at playing the piano, crafting a skill to be able to write music and play it.

*It will not feel the same. But if you are musically inclined you will take that with you and you may have a flair for writing songs and creating them. That you would take. The physical skill of playing the piano is not needed.*

So you can take the aspect of the talent that is creative?

*That is you. Yes, that is not left behind.*

Not the physical skill of quick finger work, for example.

*That is correct. The hands are tools like the brain that help you learn the skill and creative talent of playing piano.*

And that would be similar with many skills, correct?

*Yes.*

Whether you are a craftsman of some sort in pottery or painting or something.

*You would take the creativity of knowing how to put colors together, but you would not need this skill of using the brush. You could create paintings in your mind, as it were. You would not need physical skill or paint. But you would have an advantage from having worked all those times on paintings because you would have an idea of what a brush stroke looks like and you can create in your mind, without any physical skill, brush strokes on your otherworldly artwork.*

So there is still a benefit?

*Yes. But it is not necessary to have healthy hands to know how to create a painting.*

Okay. So, similarly that would work the same way with, for example, somebody who spent a lot of time learning other languages? There would not necessarily be a need to know how to speak French and Japanese, but they could still benefit.

*They would be a better communicator with different types of energy.*

So they would have the benefit of having the skill of communication, not the actual application of a language or that skill.

*Because there is no need for different languages beyond this plane. Unless you are incarnating in a different type of reality that has its own rules. But again, that would not be you, it would be a castoff of you.*

Right. That reminds me that one of the most important things I learned in college wasn't what was in the textbooks. It was learning how to learn.

*Yes, and that is very useful in any realm.*

Okay. So, why then, do people want to hang onto life in this world? Is it that addictive?

*It is a very intense experience and many are surprised at its level of intensity. It is as though you all are thrill seekers. You know those types of people that jump out of airplanes and get tattoos. That is you guys. You are all thrill seekers. Now, you may think that some of you are meek and wish to stay home and play with the cats and read a book, but from the perspective of the plane from which you came, the experience is so intense it is considered to be quite thrilling you see, and dangerous in a way, because of its intensity.*

I think you mentioned before that we are the courageous souls.

*Yes. You must be brave or have some type of bravado to embark on this type of journey in this earthly plane of existence. It is not for the faint of heart or for those whose energy has not fully developed enough to handle it. Nevertheless, some will try who are not very equipped, and will die quickly in the womb or shortly thereafter, sometimes because the experience is too intense and the soul may feel it is not ready for this type of experience. It is as though it goes up in the airplane with a parachute but chooses not to jump until next time.*

Right. So we must be a lot braver than I thought. I've seen many people who persevere under extreme circumstances when I think I would have just thrown in the towel. I know others who are braver than I am.

*Perhaps, but you are all much braver souls than most of you think you are.*

---

*Also, we did want to make it clear that any of you who are attached to each other in this physical realm can continue to have as close a relationship as you desire when you pass through this reality and on to the next step.*

That makes me smile.

*It should be of comfort to many of you. Relationships are very important on this planet. In fact, they are the most important thing you have on this planet and for good reasons.*

Relationships are the most important thing that we have on this planet?

*That is correct.*

Wait, it's not money?

*(Laughing) It is not money! Even those who desire great wealth and seek it all their lives will only miss the relationships and not the money, you see. When you pass on to the next reality, you may have a mansion if you choose and it doesn't cost any money. Only your creativity and imagination are required. You do not have to buy a lot on which to build your house. You will create one if that is what you desire or you can simply live in no time and no space with no mansion. Money matters not. What matters is the love that you make, that you take, and that you create on this plane.*

And we get to take the love and relationships with us?

*Yes. So do not fear. All of you mortals shall be reunited in immortality if that is your wish.*

I'm sure that is a wish for a lot of people.

*It certainly is. And many are more than pleased to find that their loved ones are available to them.*

There is a huge recurring theme of lamenting all of the things that people never got a chance to say to those loved ones before they crossed over.

*Yes, and it is beneficial to say what you need to say to the person before they cross over because you could spend the rest of your life lamenting it. However, once you have done your own crossing over you will be able to say these things to them, although they will already know.*

They will already know? So it is just for our own benefit?

*Yes, it is only for your benefit and for the benefit of the person who is hearing while they are still on this plane. They will know how you feel when they cross.*

So, if you have any misunderstandings with somebody, when you reunite with them after crossing over the misunderstandings will pretty much go away, correct?

*Yes, all will be understood. All is understood.*

So, when you reconnect with somebody it's always on the premise that there are no hard feelings, everyone understands why the other person did what they did and said what they said? It seems as though what you are telling me is that there are no grudges to be held because everyone understands.

*Yes, no grudges, however there are still some of those adversarial relationships of which I spoke. But there is not a grudge or a misunderstanding, there is perhaps an evaluation of the adversarial relationship and its effectiveness. There may be a decision to avoid each other and try again for resolution. But with those you love there are no misunderstandings to clear up. You will understand their motives and they will understand yours, and in the light of pure love all is forgiven.*

That is comforting. I envisioned someone getting slapped by someone waiting for them as soon as they crossed over. But I see that is not likely to happen.

*That doesn't happen unless it is some sort of welcome inside joke as an expression of love. However, you will also know if there was someone who was pretending to like you who never liked you, and vice versa.*

Because you'll be able to see through the deception that was portrayed here.

*That is correct. There is no deception except for those who choose to incarnate in certain realities with certain rules, like your earthly realm that allows for such fantasies as deception.*

Now, I understand a deception is a fantasy on the grandest scale of things. But is there still actually real deception here? I mean, if I had a secret that I am keeping from someone, do they actually know on some higher level?

*On some level, yes. Their larger entity will know, though the incarnate personality may not acknowledge it their whole lives.*

Will their larger entity rat me out and tell my secret?

*No. Only if it is beneficial to the personality involved.*

And how would that work? Would they get some sort of suspicion?

*They would. Yes. Because they know on some level, but only if it is beneficial for them to know. There are girls who are hopelessly in love with men who are not in love with them but are married to them nonetheless. These girls do not wish to know that their men are not hopelessly in love with them. They will choose to believe the lie until they die.*

Right. But if they had at any moment stopped feeling that way they might realize rather quickly that their man is sleeping with someone else?

*Yes, if that were the case, yes. It would be easy for them to discover it if it was something they wanted to do or if they wanted to move on to a different situation.*

Very interesting.

Okay. Is there anything else you'd like to add about relationships or soulmates?

*Just that there are relationships between entities and personalities that have been going on since anyone can remember anything, since the beginning of memory, if you will. And there are some relationships that change and fade. There are relationships here on Earth of those who wish to meet again and again and again with the same energy and they go off and coincide with other energies and then come back to the ones they love. This happens quite frequently. So, if you do have a romantic idea of a soul mate, and I'm telling you that this is a fantasy, it is not impossible that you are not a couple of these "from-the-beginning-of-time" energies that wish to be consistently together.*

*But again, I stress that it is a choice, a continuous choice for both of the parties involved. There is no law that says they must be together forever. There is no, "I am half of the soul and you are the other half." You are soul-fragments of many fragments of a larger soul. But there are energies that continually come together again and again and again and if it is your wish, you can be one of these energies. There are, what could be called, soul-friends.*

*There are also those energies that jump into different relationships with other energies every single incarnation. They have a hunger for different types of relationship experiences and they wish to have all manner of relationships they can possibly think of. They will have relationships with lovers of different sex, of the same sex, of all different persuasions. Now, these types of incarnate personalities generally have many dear friends and they skip around a lot throughout their life.*

*There are other energies that stick with sort of a family group and incarnate with the same group again and again and again, and so it is as though they are soul-friends with several different people. And of course there are the family relationships like the obligatory father-son, mother-daughter relationships, as well as sibling relationships. These may be groups of souls that are close and they incarnate again and again in many different roles and relationships. You may recognize yourself in this group of energy. But it is up to the individual energy which type he or she wishes to be, because all experience is open to you, if you wish it.*

That's very interesting.

*It is possible that you could be a different type of energy with a different type of relationship group. There are too many to list here and if you happen to belong to a different group, I apologize for neglecting to describe your ilk.*

So when you say they incarnate again and again, that is still under the idea that two soul-fragments could be married in life and maybe in another incarnation they will both spawn freshly minted souls that might then be close friends in their own lives.

*Yes. That is correct.*

Each time is a new freshly minted soul-fragment. Like we talked about in the reincarnation chapter, it is still not a re-using of the same soul.

*It is not a re-using of the same soul, it is a freshly minted soul-fragment created from you. So you see, it is like this new soul-fragment is your child and you have a great interest in seeing this soul do well and watching it and participating with it. For you, Robert, I know you are very interested in your cat, Stitch, for instance, and you love to watch him and see him happy and see him grow. It is similar to this but it is an even deeper connection. But there is the same type of love there for your creations, for your freshly minted castoff souls. They are of you.*

*So for example, after you die you might say to your beloved energy or soul-friend who walks beside you in many instances, "Let us have 'children' or soul-fragments together. Let us have a man and a woman or a woman and a woman or any suitable combination who will be together in this coming life. Let us create these children and cast them together and watch them and participate with them in their experiences."*

Okay. Then we might even invite the entity of the cat that we knew from a previous life to create a new kitten soul-fragment at some point?

*Yes, absolutely. There are many types of energies this cat could create to participate with the two of you.*

All this importance placed on relationships makes me feel like I shouldn't spend so much time alone.

*Is that the case? Do you feel you spend too much time alone? Because you are not really alone. None of you ever are.*

Not always, but sometimes. Focusing on relationships with other people seems to be very rewarding sometimes. Although, it is often stressful. But with the right people it's really great.

*Of course. But if they are truly friends of yours, they will remain so in this life and beyond. They will not disappear, if you love them.*

# CHAPTER 10
## YOUR CHEERLEADING SECTION

In this chapter, Brahma relates to us the numerous types of beings who are cheering us on in our lives from the sidelines. Greater entities, spirit guides, and angels who watch over us are all part of this fan club. We get a little insight into how to communicate with our fan club and how they communicate with each other and us.

---

The title of this chapter implies that it has something to do with encouraging others. How does this relate to our relationships with others?

*It has to do with relationships you possess on my plane of reality, the plane you shall return to, that you do return to often at night and after you pass over. There are literally scads of beings who stand by and assist you, and they want you to do well and they cheer you on. Most people have no idea how many beings are interested in them, are counting on them, and are cheering for them. It is as though you are a football star at the Super Bowl and there are so many beings surrounding you cheering you on and wanting you to do well. These beings differ in energy type and in species type.*

*You and most mortals have heard of angels or the seraphim. They are one species of energy that does not ever incarnate. And you have a team of these cheering you on. You also have friends, colleagues, what you would term as spirit guides, teachers, and other friends who watch you and want you to do well. It is important to them that you do well because it contributes to the expansion and happiness of all. And you were one of the ones that chose to come to this very difficult arena. It is something like a very difficult and challenging physical football game. They cannot or do not feel up to the task of taking it on themselves. But they will watch you do it and cheer you on for the good of all.*

Okay. So, you are saying we don't realize how many fans we have?

*That is correct. If some of you realized how many fans, as you put it, you have you would certainly be less lonely, never desolate, never depressed. You are often cutting yourself off from the knowledge, the help, and the assistance of these other beings. You fantasize that you are alone in this, that you are not connected to anyone else who cares. This is not the case. There are thousands of beings who care what happens to you every day.*

How do we not cut ourselves off from their help? How do we receive the help? How do we sense them or feel their support?

*You need to quiet the chitter-chatter of your mind. One way to do this is to meditate daily and focus on your breathing to get your brain into the habit of quieting down minimizing unnecessary electrical activity. The brain sends you all kinds of crazy messages that interfere with the mind's ability to communicate with its source and those beings who are nonphysical. The brain is constant with its physical input. The mind is not physical. You must quiet the brain so that you can hear what's going on in the mind. Even during the day if you do not wish to take time to meditate, if you focus on your breathing and quiet the chitter-chatter and try to focus on opening your mind, you may be able to hear messages or encouragement or ideas from outside yourself from the beings who are with you, who are very often trying to help you. It is as though you are the football star on television, and your fans are yelling at the television screen trying to help you and tell you what to do, and you cannot hear it. It is as though you are alone, but you are not.*

But you're saying there is a way to hear this encouragement?

*There is a way unlike with a television screen analogy. There is a way to hear.*

Is it just that we "football players" are so focused on playing that we ignore all of the input and encouragement?

*Yes, that is correct.*

Continuing the analogy, if the players listen to the encouragement, they can be more successful?

*Yes, very often if they can understand it, if it makes sense to them, it will help them do well. The energy alone projected from these beings toward you, if you would accept it, would help you. But you must accept it. They cannot foist it upon you without your permission.*

Okay. So these cheerleaders come in all varieties?

*Yes, many different types of energies are interested in your journey.*

Don't they have their own things that they're doing?

*They do. But your life is a very specific and special type of manifestation and contributes—in some ways with more gravity than other types of experiences—to the expansion of all-that-is. Because it is such a dense experience, it accelerates expansion. These energies may not feel they can accelerate as fast, so they count on you to play the game for them to help them be more of who they want to become.*

Do the different types of these cheerleaders or fans have different contributions to my success? For example, you mentioned angels. Do they have a certain ability that, say, spirit guides do not have? Using the sports analogy, is there a particular assistant coach that excels in defensive stuff and a coach whose specialty is something else and they both have different types of information that players need to listen to?

*Yes, all sorts of beings contribute not only to you who have incarnated, but often to each other as well and to many other types of non-physical beings.*

*Spirit guides are those energies who agreed to assist you before you're incarnated. Those are beings you know, that you have known, and generally have an agreement with. They said, "I will be there to point you in the right direction, and to try and help you." And you understood this and agreed to it before you were born. Spirit guides are often those you were very close to in another experience.*

*Angels on the other hand affect us and your species in a different way. Their energy is softer but sometimes more pointed. If there is an emergency situation, say a situation where there was going to be an automobile wreck, and they know it is not the intention of the souls involved to leave this plane, they can assist. Accidents can occur if a soul attracts them [accidents] to itself, or is not paying attention. Angels have the ability to step in. They can stop a moving vehicle, things of this nature. Generally their energy is very soft but they can actually manipulate physical matter for short periods of time. This is a very special ability that spirit guides do not have.*

And you mentioned angels are a type of energy that has never actually incarnated as a human?

*They have never incarnated. That is not their path. They love us very much. They look on at us with love and compassion and they do not speak to us so much as send us energy. They send us loving energy, and when they try to speak to us they speak to us in thoughts and not in words. They communicate in inclinations. We might think, "Oh I think I'll go over there." And not, "Someone just told me to go over there."*

You said us. Does that mean they affect non-physical beings such as yourself as well as physical beings like me?

*Yes, that is correct. They are interested in us all. They are very interested in us because we contribute to their expansion. They would never incarnate. It is not in their nature. In a way you can say they are like pets. Not to belittle them, but then I would not like to belittle pets either. Both serve their function. Both are loving energies that surround us that want the best for us. Only with angels, they do possess that certain power to interrupt in the physical world if necessary. They can sometimes manifest themselves as humans for brief periods of time as well. This is not to be confused with incarnation. They will disappear after they are finished. They will not have a continuing life if they manifest. It will just be briefly to impart some important information or to stop something or to make something happen. If the angels decide to interfere it is always taken under counsel first. There is a large group of energies that will agree to this interference, and agree that it is necessary and best for all. They will not just jump in without the consent of everyone, including your larger entity. Your larger entity cannot step in the way an angel can, but it can give consent for an angel to do so.*

Now is this the same type of angel that people have reported seeing? Or perhaps some version of an angel? Maybe some people are not experts in other-world entity identification, but is that the same idea, where they have appeared in momentous and important occasions of history?

*Yes. Angels are what you call them. They do not mind the title. They do not particularly ascribe to a title. But this is what people are referring to, this type of energy that is benevolent that "hangs around" to assist.*

Okay.

*Spirit guides, on the other hand, will talk to you. You may not feel the inclination to act. It will be like you heard a voice instructing you to act. Do you see? It is a different type of communication.*

Okay. And you mentioned friends and colleagues and I imagine acquaintances and family members of a sort are all rooting for us as well?

*Yes. Everyone that you have known in this life and in previous lives who you have been close to, and there are many, are on your side watching you, rooting for you, hoping that you do well, that you find happiness, that you find expansion, that you find excitement and creativity. They are all hoping that you create more ideas for them to expand upon.*

Okay. Now, some of these cheerleaders are people who have incarnated and are here with me now?

*Yes.*

Like friends?

*Yes.*

Now, is there more to that than we actually see? When a person is encouraging another to do something or to be successful, is there more to it than just what we see as far as encouragement in cheerleading? Say I have a friend who is struggling with something and I am attempting to encourage him to do something or help him, and there are obvious things that I am doing that are helping him. But is there more to it than meets the eye because of my intention? Am I helping him in ways that I am not really aware of? Perhaps through spirit guides?

*Because you are energetically wishing him well? Yes, of course. Of course this is the case. If you wish anything well and put your energy towards it, you are assisting. You are sending benevolent energy. The energy must be accepted by the receiver and this can happen consciously or, as you like to say, unconsciously. Though generally, this acceptance is really just conscious in the larger entity and not so much in the smaller one. But the more good feelings that are put towards this friend you wish to encourage, the more positive energy this friend has access to draw upon if needed, if wanted. When you send love to a creature or fellow being, this helps them even if you never tell them you have done this. They will recognize you. If you do not know them, when they see you they will feel a kinship because you have been sending them love. They will know you in a way that is not the normal physical way of knowing you. They will be interested in getting to know you, if is the case, on the physical plane as well. Is this understood?*

I think so, yes. Is it better to encourage people to be successful and let them have that experience than it would be to do something for them? Sometimes it seems like we like to help people but sometimes it seems like it might be better to let them struggle and help themselves.

*Sometimes it is necessary for their growth to do it themselves. Sometimes you can see that if you just did this one thing for them they would soar in other ways. But they are stuck perhaps. So it is entirely dependent upon the situation and the individual.*

That's what I thought. I am trying to understand the way in which we receive energy or encouragement from these spiritual cheerleaders as well as other physical friends.

*Some of these cheerleaders have more access to you than others. The spirit guides and the angels, for instance, have a little more access to you than other types of beings who are cheering you on and wishing you well. There are beings [made] purely of light that will probably never speak to you. They are not as close to you in your circle of friends, but they love you just the same.*

---

Are there animal spirit guides?

*Of course. Animals are surrounded by cheerleaders just as we are.*

I mean are there animal spirits that we would perceive as animals helping us?

*Yes, this occurs as well. There can be animals in spirit form that assist humans. There are humans who are very attached to certain types of animals, and the spirits of these animals may also assist. Requests for assistance from these guides is not required, but it is often appreciated. They may help in any case, but they appreciate the acknowledgment much like some pets appreciate acknowledgment. There are many humans with attachments to certain types of animals. There is no reason it should end on this earthly plane, you see. It continues in an exponential manner to other realities and planes to which you are connected. Your loving childhood dog who passed on is still happy to help you. Other non-human animals from relationships in other existences are available as well for guidance and encouragement.*

Is my relationship with souls who are here on this plane more important than my relationship with my cheerleaders? Should I focus more on the people around me rather than listening to my spirits? People here may seem to be more helpful, but spirits may be wiser.

*You should focus on whichever relationships give you the most satisfaction. If you are getting satisfaction from other worldly relationships then it is not a bad thing to focus on those, though you still must interact in the human world. But if it is easier for you and more satisfying to focus on relationships in this plane, then that is what you should do. There are no hard and fast rules. It is all what is best and most satisfying.*

I just know that some people have a tendency to just close themselves off and meditate and are very inwardly focused.

*Yes, this is an attempt to bridge the gap between your physical world and my world. It is an attempt to try to bring our world back into your world. This type of reclusion is not a bad thing. The separation of our realities was never intended to be as complete a separation as it often seems. These people are doing their best to try and bridge the gap and live in both worlds.*

That is a big contrast to people who are all physical and spiritually oblivious.

*Yes, there are those who are very much involved in this world only, and only focusing on this to the exclusion of everything else. There is no right or wrong way to do it. It is whatever contributes to your best expansion and satisfaction. They are both good ways.*

Okay.

*Though, we like to believe that having one foot here and one foot in, as you would term, the heavens would be a more balanced way to go and would be the most satisfying. Not to the exclusion of this world, not to the exclusion of our world.*

To have a more complete experience?

*We would like to think, we would like to suggest, that this would be the most satisfying or balanced way to go.*

More balanced?

*Yes.*

Very interesting.

Now, regarding all these supposed fans cheering me on, assuming they are nearby, how do I hear them? In order to most benefit from them, how do I read my fan mail, so to speak? How do I communicate with my fan club?

*You must recognize that they are there and listen for them. If you do not realize they are there it will be difficult for you to pick up a fan letter and read it, you see. But if you know it is there you can look for it. You can find it. You can pick it up and read it. You must quiet the brain and listen with the mind, and we understand that this concept can be difficult for many who equate the brain and the mind in the same neat, tiny, little package. However, this is not the case, and if you concentrate, you can separate the brain from the mind and listen with the mind. It just takes some practice, some willingness and some belief that you can do so. You can start by focusing on your breathing and then attempting to listen with your mind. Focusing on your breathing quiets the chitter-chatter of the brain. It does not quiet the mind.*

So you recommend meditating?

*Yes, or at least taking a few minutes to focus on your breathing before attempting to listen with your mind. You could think of this as a different type of meditation, I suppose.*

So when my mind wanders, that's not really what is happening. It's just my brain going places?

*Very often. But sometimes it is your mind. We understand it is complicated for some to distinguish, but the brain's thoughts are often inconsequential to the larger scheme of things. The mind's thoughts are expansive, more joyful, deeper.*

So is there a way to try to distinguish those? It would be helpful to know which thoughts to toss out and which ones to focus on.

*Yes. Ask yourself, "What type of thought is it?" If you are thinking about tomorrow's laundry, I can pretty much guarantee that you are not thinking with your mind but with your brain. The mind does not care about the laundry.*

Okay.

---

Now, when people find themselves talking to angels, it is usually considered to be praying. Is praying a good method of communicating to our fan club?

*Praying is quieting the consciousness and focusing on the spiritual mind or mind consciousness. It works the same way as the meditating we spoke of.*

Now, if I am praying to angels, I'm probably not going to hear them speak to me unless they appear to me physically and speak, correct? They would probably just give me inclinations of doing something?

*Yes, you would have inclinations to follow.*

But can I also pray to a spirit guide or teacher or a friend who has passed on and listen for a response?

*Yes, absolutely.*

So that would be more of a mental dialogue. Right?

*That is correct. Though they can help you in nonverbal ways as well. The spirit guides and your friends are more like your energy than angels are. And since you are verbal creatures on this plane, sometimes they will engage you in this play. Our energies are interested in language and words. We do not find it necessary but it is a fun game. It is kind of like your video games that you like to play, not the complex involved ones but more like the simple, silly ones.*

Sort of like an exercise or a puzzle?

*Something fun to do.*

Something fun but not necessary. Right?

*Yes, but it is fun and interesting, all the same.*

So, we have spoken about different kinds of cheerleaders: friends, colleagues, spirit guides, teachers, and angels. I have heard a lot about different types of angels and I was hoping we could talk about those a little more. Are angels assigned to us? Does each individual have an angel assigned to them? How does that work?

*You all have angels that work with you. The angels do choose you to watch over, but it is a mutually chosen situation. Some angels work with more than one individual but you all have individual angels that work just with you. You and the angel both choose this relationship. And even when you are sharing the angels, this is also chosen. Sometimes it is beneficial for an angel to watch over more than one individual as their lives may be connected in some ways or perhaps their lives are similar enough that the angel can learn that what works with one individual on Earth will work for the other one as well. It is as much a learning process for them as being on this plane of existence is for you. They are not perfect either. There is trial and error. Though, they are better at some things than you are and vice versa, of course.*

Okay. So the angels' job is to watch us. Do they just sit around and watch us like watching TV? Is that their primary role?

*They have other realities and activities that they participate in, but a very good portion of their time is spent with you. That is not their only role but it is a very important role.*

So they're kind of like on call, like a doctor?

*In a way. It is sort of like it is their job so it is much of their focus. There will always be angels with you, however. Do not think that you ever walk alone because everyone is taking a break or off of their shift. There will always be at least a couple of angels with you at all times.*

So there are that many angels?

*Yes.*

Now, is there an extra supply of angels for all the people that haven't been born yet?

*Angels continue to multiply exponentially as does the energy that you are.*

So angels create more angels like themselves?

*Yes, and they are also created by you.*

You mean by my larger self, my larger entity?

*Yes. The energy of all-that-is and all its many probabilities and the very many different angels create more, you see. Creation is started by ideas. Ideas create a reality when they are more cemented. If there is a need for more angels they will come into existence.*

So, as an example: Robert lives here. He dies and crosses over. He realizes he would like to experience something and he creates a new soul who is born into a situation that is conducive to what Robert wants to experience or what the larger collective entity of Robert or Shalkeera wants to experience. Robert says, "Okay, I'm going to spawn this new soul, but I also need to supply some angels for this soul as well." Is this how it works?

*Robert's larger entity, Shalkeera, has access to a steady supply of angels. Shalkeera knows many angels. Shalkeera has many friends you see, who are angels. And they would be ready and waiting for a new soul, a new incarnation.*

I see. So did you make angels for your incarnated soul-fragments?

*Angels were already available for them.*

You just called up your angel friends at some "angel employment agency"?

*In a sense. There is an energy match that occurs. When we thought of the possibility of the soul-fragment, Bronwen, incarnating on this plane, there were angel energies that we were familiar with from angel entities that freely came forth to assist this new incarnation. It was like they were drawn to the new soul. It is less of a discussion and more of an energetic magnetism, if that makes any sense.*

It does. I'm trying to think of an analogy to make things more clear. Let's say I am a parent and one of my kids is old enough to get into some legal trouble. I would just call my lawyer firm and say, "Can you send a lawyer that specializes in the kind of trouble that my son has gotten into?" Without much of a discussion, a match would be made. For example, he would get a lawyer that specializes in dealing with kids his age.

*Yes. But of course, in this case there is no phone call being made.*

Right, because your communication does not require phone calls?

*It does not even require words, although they can be used if it is desired. Generally, the angels will not answer in words, however. This is not to say that they cannot speak. They can if they choose but there's usually no need. Sometimes they manifest themselves briefly as an incarnation in order to assist, and in this case, if there is a need for them to speak, they will do so.*

Now, when a person dies or crosses over, what happens to their angels? Do they get new jobs or do they stay with the new soul that crosses over? Or do they stay watching earthly incarnations?

*There is not always the need to have angels so closely by your side when you cross over, though you may maintain some contact with them because they are your friends. Sort of like those people you went to school with that were dear to you. You may maintain contact with some of them. But since their primary role is to assist those who reside in the earthly realm, they are needed to help more there, you see. They may stay with you if it is chosen in mutual agreement or they may go forth with another soul-part of you. You see, they were attracted to you in the first place because your energy was agreeable, and so it follows that further energy coming from you would likely be agreeable to them as well. They may assist your progeny, so to speak. Although, your progeny or your soul-fragments may have their own new angels as well. I am referring to your castoffs, your newly minted soul-fragments from you or your larger entity.*

So they could be paired up with my newly created souls?

*Yes.*

So, are there different types of angels?

*Yes. There are several different orders of the seraphim. There are the greater angels who oversee others. This is not to say that they are a boss in the traditional sense that you think of here.*

They oversee other angels?

*Yes. They are there to offer council and advice. They have been around longer, and if you earthlings see these types of angels, they appear much taller and larger to you. This is not because they take up physical space. It is because they are perceived as older and more knowledgeable and wiser by not only the angels but also by you.*

Okay. And those are called greater angels?

*There are many names for them. They do not adopt their own names. They do not care for or need titles. But yes, some would refer to them this way and it would be an explanatory title.*

*There are also those angels who stick by us more closely. These types of angels "get their hands dirty" more often, whereas the greater angels keep their distance. We are inclined somewhat to refer to them as lesser angels, but this is not the case in the way that you might think of the word lesser. They are just as important as the greater angels. Their jobs are more like a fine toothed comb than a giant brush. Shall we call them finer angels?*

*There is also a more middling type of angel that sometimes comes to get their hands dirty but more often acts as an intermediary between the angels doing the hard work and the angels doing the advising or the overseeing. There are many different types in between as well, but those are the three major types: greater, middling, and finer angels.*

And the finer angels would be the ones who would be paired up with individuals here?

*That is correct.*

And they may be with more than one individual. As an individual, I would have one of these angels or would I have more than one?

*You would ordinarily have several. The middling angels more often share and the greater angels offer advice to many middling and finer angels. So, there would be perhaps many Earth individuals assigned, as you say, to these greater angels through the middle angels and the finer angels.*

Now, you mentioned that the greater angels don't really have names or titles. Do any of these other angels have names or do they just refer to themselves as angels?

*You earthlings have names that you use to sometimes refer to these angels. But they do not necessarily refer to themselves in this way.*

Some of the religions have named angels, such as Gabriel or Michael. Is Gabriel a greater angel or would that type be a finer angel?

*Gabriel would be a greater angel: a source of wisdom and counsel for other types of angels. But you must understand there is more than one Gabriel. There are many different versions of what many refer to as one specific angel. Just as there are many selves in probabilities, there are also many angels of the same seeming entity or being because they are created by you and by other angels who imagine them, if you will, into existence. One middling angel's version of Gabriel will not be the same as another's. So there will be two Gabriels in that case.*

But they would be similar, right?

*Yes, they would most certainly have similar qualities that could be agreed on by most of you. More than one greater angel will fill the role of Gabriel.*

Okay. So the finer angels would be the ones who would have the role of watching us or watching over us?

*Yes, much more closely.*

Paying attention to what's going on in our lives?

*Yes.*

And if we needed help, they would be the ones who could intervene?

*Yes, although sometimes the middle angels are permitted to do so if necessary, if a stronger hand or more knowledge is needed for the task.*

Does that mean that they have more power?

*They have more of certain types of power.*

And they all could be seen if they chose to show themselves. Correct?

*If they had the inclination and the will to do so, they can be seen, yes.*

And what do they look like?

*It depends on the individual who perceives them. Some will see them as other earthlings like themselves. Others will see them in robes with wings. It is very individual. The same angel can be seen in many different ways. Many times an angel takes on a form that you would consider to be a comfort to you. Angels do not wish to frighten you if they incarnate. They wish to get the job done as effectively as possible, and frightening you might not expedite this.*

I've heard of archangels. What are those?

*That would be a form of a greater angel.*

That makes sense. Okay. And the term, seraphim? Does that term refer to all angels?

*We are using this term to encompass all angels. Though it may not necessarily be the term that you earthlings would use.*

Right, because many different people with different mythologies use different terminology for different types of angels.

*And these mythologies are certainly valid.*

Along the lines of mythological beings, would some of the mythological creatures that people know of actually be any type of an angel? For example would a fairy be confused with an angel? They also have wings.

*Fairies are not generally angels, though you could see an angel as a fairy perhaps if it was the wish of you and your angel.*

What would a fairy be then if it is not some kind of angel?

*Generally speaking, fairies are creatures that do not live in this realm of existence. They aren't often seen by you. However, sometimes at coordination points where realities that crisscross each other and intersect, and the space between the layers is much more thin, the energy can go up and down the layers very quickly. Sometimes if you are looking for them they can be seen. But they do not exist here on this plane of existence in the way that some people would think.*

So they are basically living in another plane of reality?

*Another realm which can sometimes be reached.*

So we are just seeing into another plane of existence when we are seeing fairies. Would that be the explanation for virtually all of the mythological types of creatures that people claim to have seen?

*Yes, they exist on other planes. This is absolutely the case. Most of your mythological creatures do exist somewhere. Generally they do not exist here. Now this is not to say that they can never or have never existed here. There is a possibility that they could be discovered at one time if you all decided that you wish to have them on this plane. If everyone wished for dragons, at some point a dragon may be incarnated here. There would, of course, be a perfectly logical explanation for this. Someone would have found an ancient dragon and someone would clone the DNA of the egg and create one, or some such scientific explanation like this.*

Because existence is required to be believable?

*That is correct. Otherwise sudden incarnation is very difficult for the world to accept. Some individuals might accept it but not everyone will believe or see and so they will not have as solid a reality on this plane. They would have more of an ephemeral existence.*

You mentioned that mythological creatures can be seen through coordination points. These are places where different worlds or different realities intersect?

*Yes.*

And there we can see fairies or dragons or whatever, or basically things that really do not or cannot exist here?

*That is correct.*

Now, does that also mean that we cannot exist there in those other worlds? These points of the intersection that we can see through, can we also go through them? Can we physically cross over into them, like doorways?

*You can be seen by them in this same way that they can be seen by you. Temporary fleeting interaction is possible but neither of you can stay permanently in either world.*

Is that because the worlds are too different?

*Yes, the energy is too different to sustain interaction for a very long time. And if you go too far from the coordination point, the connection would disappear. So you see, if you are talking to a dragon and the dragon says, "Let's walk over to this tree", and you strayed from the point, the whole landscape would disappear and you would return to your original Earth coordination point. The connection would be lost.*

Now, is that because this dragon world is too different?

*The energies creating the worlds are too different, and the physics, the laws that are inherent in each world, are too different to exist at the same time.*

Now, if the worlds were similar would that then be possible?

*You now seem to be speaking of probabilities.*

I guess that is what it would be, wouldn't it?

*Yes.*

Okay.

*Now, of course, the rules and laws, as we have said before, in your world can change. And if all of humanity wished for there to be dragons, dragons would exist again. But this would take some of your physical time and energy to create this, and the laws of your world would have to change to support such creatures.*

Now, understanding that there is a difficulty in crossing over to these worlds physically, would it be possible to mentally or spiritually visit these places?

*Yes, naturally. Especially in the dream state or the hypnogogic state. It is very easy to go to these realms at that point. But then of course you must follow their physical laws and you will know that you are in a different universe because it is not like your own. For instance, being able to fly is not something allowed by the laws that apply to your physical reality. In some other realities, of course, it is perfectly acceptable.*

Okay.

*Here, flying is only for the birds.*

Okay. So it is possible to visit in a nonphysical way but not like it is in so many of our fictional stories where people literally go into other worlds.

*It could be done fleetingly. It would not last.*

Okay.

*And when you return to your physical world, you would doubt your experience. And your doubt would be confirmed by others who would also doubt it. Some people however remain steadfast and they say, "I know what I saw". This is true in many reported alien encounters.*

Oh. So it's just a fleeting experience but, nevertheless, is still an experience. Is it an actual physical experience?

*It would not have been an experience grounded in this physical reality. It could very well have been a physical experience for the body consciousness. It is possible to slip into one of these other worlds and have a physical experience that will change your physical body once to return to this world, you see. There are some people who feel they have been implanted with alien devices, and in fact their physical anatomy has changed on some level.*

But not only because their own body consciousness is affected by their own thoughts and consciousness?

*By the foray into this other world briefly.*

Right. Or possibly by the other world coming into our world?

*Yes, naturally.*

Now, these coordination points, are they just energy coordination points or are they physical locations?

*They are physical locations.*

So for some of these people that have alien experiences, perhaps maybe their house is right there physically by a place where aliens can pop in?

*Yes, this is very likely.*

They just happen to have built their house in that spot?

*Yes. Now, of course, by saying these are physical coordination points, I do not mean to discount that they are also energy points. Because, of course, there is a massive amount of energy in these coordination points.*

Okay.

*Loch Ness, of course, is one.*

Okay, so there is a physical geographical location that corresponds with a coordination point or a window to another world?

*Yes. Los Angeles is another.*

Los Angeles? So a lot of those odd looking people are not really humans?

*(Laughing) It depends on whom you see, I suppose.*

But I suppose this unusual energy of the area can have other influences on normal people.

*Yes. Unusual experiences happen in these areas and so they are identifiable. Sedona, Arizona is another such area.*

Okay. Interesting.

*So, if you want to have an otherworldly experience, it is certainly possible to seek these out and to open yourself up and be there for a long enough time for something interesting to occur. We will speak more of mythological creatures in a separate discussion.*

Okay. Thank you.

*Certainly.*

Okay. Let's get back to angels and our fan club. The idea of angels and other spiritual beings is very often linked to religion here. What about saints? Are those like angels or are they people who lived here?

*Yes, saints are beings who have incarnated. They are of your ilk. Now, there are some who continue to be prayed to that have taken on a role of watching over and attempting to assist. And so if you pray to the saints for certain virtues or help, they can sometimes answer. They are entities who have chosen to try to assist after their earthly incarnation.*

But they're not angels?

*No, they are not angels. Saints are like you. Angels are a different species, so to speak. They are not the same type of energy as you soul-fragments and they are also different from larger entities like us.*

What about the famous saints? Saint Peter, for example. Does he exist? Does he really sit up there and have the job of letting people into the afterlife?

*No, (humorously) there are those who pray to Saint Peter and there are many entities who call themselves Peter who wish to assist on your earthly plane. There are no entities who permit or revoke the right to enter heaven who are named Peter. There are not entities that do this at all. However, of course, upon passing, some of you will see Peter because you believe Peter will be there, but this will not actually be a Saint Peter. It will be your spirit guide or some of your energy that you have created to become a Peter for you. But this will not last as the spirit guide will take on its own true form, or the energy will disintegrate when you start to see the truth of where you are, which is not really at a gate where you will be permitted or denied entrance to heaven.*

Okay. I ask because it may be in the mind of a reader who is thinking about the popular concept of saints.

*Certainly. But as I said, there are many saints or guides who call themselves Peter who can be called upon to assist.*

Okay.

*There are many energies who are willing to lend a hand if called upon. This is why sometimes prayer is helpful. If you pray to a certain entity, they or perhaps another will hear you and attempt to assist if they can. It is something that many entities enjoy and appreciate doing because, as I have said, the expansion of one contributes to the expansion of all. Assistance is mutually beneficial.*

So basically, if someone just prays to anyone, it's likely someone will hear that?

*Yes, many times it is heard. It is not always answered in the way that the Earth personality would wish it to be answered, but many times it is answered in some way.*

When people pray, they might always pray to the same god or gods. Does it make a difference which god one prays to?

*Only your belief in their ability to help you would make the difference.*

Okay. So there isn't really any advantage in praying to an angel or to anybody who is listening to help me versus praying just to Zeus, for example?

*If you have a strong belief in Zeus, then we might suggest that you continue to pray to Zeus. However, if you believe Zeus cannot help you when you are cast adrift in a ship on the ocean, then perhaps Poseidon would be the better god to pray to. It is all dependent upon your belief in their ability to hear you and to help you. Because with your belief comes permission to help.*

So by having belief you are allowing help to come? You are officially accepting it?

*Yes, that is correct and it must be accepted, they cannot force their help upon you without your consent.*

So there is power in faith?

*Yes, absolutely. It does not mean that there is a real Zeus in the way they you think of him or even a real Poseidon in the way you think of him. But there are Zeuses and Poseidons and Jupiters and Neptunes and there are those entities that will take on the guise of a Zeus or a Neptune in order to help you if they hear your call.*

So all you have to do is pray and believe?

*Yes, you can pray specifically or generally, but it is your belief and acceptance of help that will help determine how much help you actually get with your request.*

If an angel hears somebody asking for help but is not serious in their request, can the angel tell the difference between somebody praying and somebody just saying I wish that would happen?

*Yes, they can tell the difference.*

Is that because it has to do with one's desire or intention?

*Yes, absolutely, and these are read by the angels more easily than you read them in each other. Remember they do not communicate in words.*

Right. So it doesn't matter exactly what you say?

*If it matters to you, if words are important to you then it is important.*

They are not going to mishear me or mistake what I say like in some comedy movie?

*No, but if you say the wrong thing it could affect the outcome dependent upon your memory of what you said and the way you think of the things that you said.*

So if there is a mistake it would be my own fault?

*Yes, essentially. There was a story Bronwen once read about a witch who had performed a spell when her husband went hunting. Now, spells are essentially prayers with a little infusion of energy in them. She cast a spell saying that he would shoot the biggest deer in the forest. The husband ventured out to hunt for food and after a short time the witch began to wonder about his success. The witch realized that she had not been specific in the spell and that she should have clarified that the deer would be killed quickly. The husband did actually shoot the biggest deer in the forest, but the deer got away. The deer was only superficially harmed. So the woman realized that she had made the spell to shoot the biggest deer, but her lack of belief in the effectiveness of the spell allowed for it [the deer] to survive the shooting. She recognized this mistake and she made a vow to be more careful with her words in her spells.*

So, she wasn't thinking when she made her request. Especially since her prayer was in the form of a spell where she believed the words that are chosen have significant importance. Her belief in the wording is what affected the outcome. Right?

*Yes, the belief in the words of the prayer or spell or request for spiritual help can influence the effectiveness.*

When people pray for something and they actually have a prayer answered, why do they sometimes insist so crazily that this is proof of their god's existence or righteousness, when anybody can pray for any reason to any god or spirit and get the same result?

*You're asking me about human nature?*

Yes. Don't laugh, but sometimes I do not understand it.

*Well, you know the ego has a desire to be right, to prove that it is valid, that what it believes is valid.*

But from what you are telling me, everybody is correct. Everyone can pray in their own way and it can be answered.

*That is true, in a sense. Although you might be more correct to pray to your own entity, your spirit guides, your angels, or anybody who might be listening who was willing to lend a hand than to pray to a specific god that you worship or idolize.*

*Idol worship is not necessary. It is belittling to the worshipper. You are not so lesser that you must get down on your knees and pray to some looming god who is so much greater than you. And if you believe this, you are putting more power in the hands of this god than in your own hands. It seems more beneficial if you accept your own power and greatness. You can affect changes yourself more quickly if you believe this.*

Okay. Now, since it appears as though there are different angels or spirit guides that may be more specifically equipped to help out with some particular situation, how would one know whom to pray to? For example, would I pray to a different angel if I needed an answer to some question as opposed to needing something to happen? It seems like different specific things to pray about might require praying to different angels.

*It doesn't matter so much to whom you pray. However, a spirit guide might be more suited to give advice. Angels might be more suited to give assistance. Gods might be more suited to deliver miracles. It might be helpful were you to imagine some of your angels or spirit guides and consciously give them names and personalities. This, you see, would not be completely your imagination, though you may think it was. You would be picking up on character traits and you would be more in touch with the so-called super powers they may have to assist you. And if you named them and gave them certain traits, then you would know whom to pray to; you would solidify them and it might be an easier connection for them to help you because you have put them to the forefront of your mind. It is all an energy, a thinking, an idea connection, you see.*

Right. That's what I was thinking. It seems like it would be easier if I had an idea of a counselor who is really good at dealing with relationship problems, for example. Then if I could just pray to this "marriage counselor spirit guide" it would be easier for me to believe in their ability to help me.

*Yes, it can help some of you to personify and flesh out your helpers. It can be easier to connect with them that way. This is why many religions and belief systems do it for you. But you are perfectly capable of creating your own personifications of helpers and aides. They do not mind what you call them, only that you know of them. They would bask in gratitude at your acknowledgment of them.*

Also, it doesn't seem practical to pray to your god of war if you have problems with your spouse.

*No. But if you are trying to win a battle this would be a better scenario.*

Right. So, how much you believe in their ability to help seems to have a huge impact on how helpful it is to pray. Correct?

*Yes, naturally. There are armies of help. Since you brought up war we will call them armies. There are armies of those aides who are ready to assist you. There is no shortage of helpers.*

So, I can just imagine a particular adviser and their abilities and I might be able to name this adviser, and they just might be whispering to me their name and the nature of their personality to help my imagination.

*Yes, that is correct.*

And would they actually tell me their name? Or is that up to me because they don't really go by names? Is that correct?

*They do not care so much what they are called. They might suggest something to you, however, that you might both be comfortable with. They will not be insulted by any particular name.*

Can I also ask someone like you? Can you give me a name of somebody that I personally could pray to?

*Certainly. Since you are speaking of counselors, there is a male energy around you whose name through my connection sounds like Jessop.*

(I was simply asking if this was possible. I was not expecting Brahma to actually identify my angels and spirit guides. But since this is how the conversation went, I thought it might be an interesting example of a "cheerleading section".)

And what is his specialty?

*He is a specialty of advice and wisdom. He is sage and tries to point you in the right direction when you are confused. He tries to give you inclinations to do what is going to be best for your evolution, your life's purpose, and your happiness. He is an angel who has not incarnated. He is a finer angel.*

That is great to know.

*He would be thrilled for some sort of acknowledgment.*

So could I ask him about other helpers that are available to me?

*Yes, of course.*

You mentioned before that angels sort of give inclinations and spirit guides or friends or colleagues who have passed on would be more likely to have sort of a mental dialogue.

*Yes.*

So if I wanted to ask a question that may have an answer rather than an inclination or direction it might be better to ask one of them?

*Yes, a spirit guide might be best for that or perhaps a relative whom you trust who has passed. Or even those incarnational friends that you are not currently aware of in this life.*

Right. Can you give me the name of a spirit guide?

*Give us a moment.*

Okay.

*A spirit guide is Reginald for you. You have three about you who very closely work with you. There are others who drop in and out. Reginald is a primary spirit guide.*

Reginald. And there are others?

*You are asking for another name?*

Well, okay. Sure. Can you give me a name?

*There are three main spirit guides in your aura. There are others who drop in and out.*

Okay. And Reginald is the primary one?

*Yes. Reginald is an incarnational friend, a blood-brother so to speak. He has agreed to help look after you in this life. You have done the same for him on different occasions.*

Okay.

*You have a "Wendy" about you as well.*

Wendy?

*A spirit guide. She says it is Wende with and an E not with a Y. I believe she is joking in a sarcastic way about being specific about the spelling.*

I see. I do tend to relate to sarcastic people. Thank you. I know that the power of prayer and faith is used to help a lot of people in finding direction and in connecting to their source energy. I haven't relied much on prayer but I may start to explore this. Thank you for the names.

*Yes, indeed. You could find them for yourself or names that suited you more if you liked, however, since you asked I have provided what I perceive from my viewpoint.*

Okay. And if I was really desperate and needed a god, I should pray to my larger entity, Shalkeera, for example?

*Shalkeera may be your closest idea to a god. However, if you like, you can create one.*

I can just create a god?

*If you like.*

Okay. I guess, why not? A lot of religions have done this, right?

*Absolutely. Your god would be no less valid than Zeus. Although your god might take some time to build up the same amount of energy.*

That is understandable.

Now, we have spoken about spirit guides, angels, and even gods. What about the type of spiritual being that is unhelpful or contrary? I'm thinking of the idea of demons. Do they fall into the mythical creature category or are they real?

*Demons are thought forms created by you. They are created from fear and from anxiety and even hatred. They seem to have a lot of power because of the energy that you have put into them. But they are less powerful than your own entity, your own energy, or the angels and spirit guides that serve you because they are, in some ways, not real. Thoughts and thought forms, of course, are valid and real, but because demons are not anchored in love they will disperse quickly if the source of them is discovered or if their disguise is pulled off, so to speak.*

Okay. So they are only dangerous with respect to how much power we give them?

*This is correct and should be dealt with and recognized as such.*

Are you saying they are all a part of the individual who perceives them?

*Yes.*

They are not some independent creation coming to get you?

*No, they can be created by others as well but you must share in their creation in order for them to affect you. The teacher, Seth, gave some very good advice for those encountering thought forms such as demons. You address the dark form that is scary and frightening and you say to it, "May peace be with you." Often it will go on its way.*

Okay. So they're not at all like angels?

*No, they are not a species. They are self-created.*

They are not fallen angels?

*No.*

Okay.

*There is only love at the truth of things, you see. These thought forms are not created by any such energy.*

Okay.

*And, even if they gathered enough energy for a somewhat permanent creation, they would have to evolve and enlighten, you see, because such is the way of things. You cannot have an energy being that will not evolve and enlighten. It must occur. There is no energy being created that will not climb up the spiritual scale, you see.*

So if it does that, then it will become less of a dark energy?

*Yes, it will transform. And this is only if it garners enough energy to become its own creation. Most often they do not. But you see, if it has garnered this energy it will inherently have changed into something that will enlighten and evolve.*

Okay.

Now since angels can sometimes incarnate in a physical form in our physical reality, can other entities do that? For example, do you have a physical form?

*I can take a physical form if I wish.*

By creating a soul fragment or just appearing?

*I appear to Bronwen in a state that you do not see, in an area that you do not see. I create a human representation of myself for her.*

Okay.

*I could do it on this plane perhaps if the conditions were right. It would take a lot of focus and energy.*

Okay. Now, even though you don't have a physical manifestation here, do you see what is going on here or do you only get that through what Bronwen sees?

*I get it through all of my soul fragments. I soak up the information as the leaves soak up the sunlight and the rain for the trees. So there is information coming at me from many, many places at once.*

But you don't receive it directly? I mean, we have this idea that people from the spirit world—personalities, entities, and people like you—can watch over us and know what is going on.

*We know what is going on through you.*

But you don't necessarily see stuff that we don't see?

*Not necessarily unless we are contacted by an angel or a spirit guide.*

Can they see stuff?

*Yes, of course.*

So angels have the ability to watch what is going on?

*Yes, of course.*

Okay. So if somebody doesn't see a bus coming, you wouldn't know it but an angel probably would?

*I might feel the bus as a gopher feels an earthquake coming. I might understand that it was going to come, especially if it was going to affect one of my soul fragments. I wouldn't necessarily see it in the same physical way that you would see it.*

Right, but you could see it if somebody you were connected with saw it, because you have many sources of information and many eyes watching?

*Yes of course.*

Okay.

*And you must also understand that the past, present, and future are one to me and so if a bus is coming and going to run over one of my soul fragments, I will know it. Not only will I feel it perhaps, but I will know it because it has already occurred in a probable future.*

Because you will have seen it or will learn about it because one of your personalities would have learned about it by being hit by the bus and you can get the information from her probable future self?

*Yes, this is correct.*

Okay.

*My sources of information are complex, but I would like to say (humorously) that my spies are everywhere!*

Right, because we always wonder that. Is somebody watching me or watching over me?

*Your angels and spirit guides are watching.*

And I imagine that they convey information.

*Yes, angels can intervene on your behalf. They can speak to each other and they can speak to your larger entity if necessary.*

Okay. Now, can dead people appear physically here?

*Yes.*

As themselves? Or as other creatures? How can we see them?

*They most often appear as themselves and some people can see them. It takes quite a bit of effort in order to manifest oneself in an earthly plane from another plane if one has not decided to incarnate, which, by the way, takes quite an effort in itself. However, doing it just for a moment as the human they once were takes a tremendous amount of energy from the personality. It also takes an open mind and a great desire on the receiving-end human personality wanting to see this crossed-over individual. It does not happen often, but it does happen.*

Can they appear as other creatures or would that be just as difficult?

*They can send a part of their consciousness into an animal such as a bird or some other creature. Very often birds are chosen for this purpose. Their consciousness is very light and free and they do not feel so territorial about their bodies. If another (non-physical) energy wishes to join them they do not often feel threatened by this, and so it is easy to send energy to one of these creatures and have it accepted. It may be incorporated, or maybe the energy will leave after it has done what it has come to do. Humans however, are very territorial. These energies could not often penetrate another human unless the human willingly and knowingly allowed it.*

In that case would it be like channeling?

*Indeed, it would. But if they wish to make their presence known to convince the human left behind that they continue on, often they would attempt to take their own form. If this is not possible in the material plane, it is certainly possible in the dream plane. And many times people will awaken convinced that they have spoken with the dead, and in this case, they have.*

Okay, another question. I was curious about getting advice as inclinations from angels and getting help from spirit guides. What category would advice like a premonition fall under? When people get premonitions, would that be an angel giving us a glimpse of what might happen?

*It can depend on the form that the premonition takes. If it is a voice premonition, it is most likely from a spirit guide. A vision premonition could be from an angel. However, it can also happen when the energy of the person opens up to the true* nature of time, to the greater timeline, to the energy of events and receiving the premonition. This can happen without any assistance from a guide and is just the opening up of one's own energy perspective.

So it's possible to just catch a glimpse of a future probable situation not necessarily as a result of somebody whispering in your ear what is going to happen?

*This is correct. Although, of course it can happen with assistance as well.*

So there is some validity to premonitions?

*Yes, of course. It seems surprising that any of you would question this. But I do understand there is a sort of superstition that is looked down upon in your society and sometimes you label these things as superstition and sometimes, of course, they are. But many good premonitions are thrown away in the name of superstition.*

Right, because a premonition may come true, but it is actually a probable situation so it may not necessarily come to pass, and it could be averted. Right?

*Yes, it can always be changed.*

So if the situation changes and the vision doesn't occur, then people would say that it was nothing and wasn't a premonition at all.

*Yes, this is correct.*

So maybe that is why they don't place any value on it.

*But these things should always be noted, because even in the case of a superstition or a fear, the fear needs to be addressed. Otherwise, the situation feared could still come to pass. It needs to be dealt with.*

Is that because the not dealing with it could cause a sort of thorn in your side to fester or become more painful so that it actually gets more energy directed towards it?

*Well, it is like that perhaps. It is like a seed that is planted that will grow if you do not pluck it out of the ground and uproot it. If you ignore it, it may not grow or it may grow anyway because it has already been planted and is not impeded. Your temporary crisis may be averted, but what is causing the fear can still affect the future probability.*

Okay.

*The cause of the fear needs to be discovered, and in your linear-like pattern of time perception, it is often helpful to reason it away, to understand ways it could be false, and to start to find ways to believe that it is false. Now, if there is a fear that is very, very deep-rooted, it may not be possible to avert a fearful premonition, therefore it can be a preview of things to come, and it may come true. However, if you try to deal with that in some way it could perhaps lessen the consequences.*

*The only reason a premonition would be given to you by yourself or by others is so you could heed it and change something. You will not often be given a premonition of something you can do nothing about in any way.*

Okay. I figure at the very least you could prepare yourself for the future situation. Right?

*This is, of course, correct. It could lessen an emotional dramatic impact to the spirit or the body consciousness.*

Okay, thanks.

I'm out of questions about the cheerleading section. Is there anything you would like to add?

*We want you all to understand how much you are valued, how much you are loved and how many others are cheering for you and counting on you. You would have many boxes and boxes of fan mail to read if you could. You will understand more when you cross over and have assimilated your experience here and have accepted your new reality. There is no reason for any of you to ever feel alone. You are not. You are loved and appreciated by many no matter who you are. Many entities want the best for you and want you to do well and they love you without limits.*

That is very good to know. Thank you.

*Certainly.*

It always feels good to be loved.

*As I have said, Love is the force that propels the universe.*

# CHAPTER 11
## HUMAN EVOLUTION

In this discussion, Brahma gives us insight into how our current state of spiritual evolution has come to be and some of the reasoning behind the current relationship between our souls and our larger entities, and with our physical bodies and our normal consciousness. We also get a glimpse of the direction that our spiritual evolution is headed and with it, the physical evolution that may occur because of it.

*We are pleased to be in your audience this evening.*

Welcome back Brahma.

*Thank you very much. It is good to speak with you again.*

The next chapter is Human Evolution.

*Yes.*

Human evolution can have different meanings: A physical or biological evolution and a spiritual evolution. My immediate guess is that we are going to talk about both. Is that correct?

*Yes, we would like to speak about the evolution of the human race, of the creatures that have chosen to incarnate on this planet and their spiritual line of evolution.*

So, our discussion is with more emphasis on a spiritual evolution?

*Yes. When entities first decided to have an incarnation, you may consider this to be many millions of years ago or thousands of years ago depending upon your belief system, we were quite a different type of energy than we are now. The incarnations were different. The line between us and you was not as separate and distinct as it is now. There was not then this feeling of separatism. Also, the tactile sensations and the ability to evolve quickly were not as developed back then. So we had to choose* what to sacrifice to get more experience, and this led to the development of the ego. It was a different type of existence that I shall try to explain. It has led to where you are now spiritually and it is headed in yet a further direction. You are not at the end of the course, so to speak. The evolution has continued into the future of the earthly experience.

Can you tell me about how it all started?

*We will attempt to describe it in a manner, basic to our understanding of course, that is presentable to you.*

All right.

*We have always been wanting to evolve. We cannot remember a time when we were idle and not wishing to evolve. We understand that there is a Big Bang theory where, in spiritual terms, God discovers itself and says something like, "I think, therefore I am." But we do not remember this if it occurred. It is possible, but we do not remember a time when we were not active. This was part of an experiment, and we have been experimenting with ideas and worlds and types of incarnations for as long as we can remember.*

*This idea began with a desire for a more complete experience, a more immersive experience. It is similar in a way to when you were playing Atari and you had a desire to play today's immersive, 3D, high-graphics video games. We wanted to be more involved and more distracted, and we wanted for it to be a more complete experience because we felt that with this more immersive experience we could evolve faster. And like you on this plane, we are always looking for a better faster car, a better faster computer. This is our nature. This is why this occurs. This is why you have science and technology. It is because it is in our nature to always improve and we wish to have evolution as quickly as we can. It is wonderful fun for us.*

*So, at first we designed a more primitive type of world. You may think of it as the cave-man days if you wish. But it was a world where we were very in touch with ourselves. It is a bit more like you playing video games where you are controlling a character through adventures. It is mostly a third person perspective where you are always in contact with your character. Your character is always in contact with you. And you do not often forget that you are playing a game. So we were exploring this world and we were in constant communication with our source. Our energy fragments we sent to this world to explore always felt at home and safe and happy and knew that nothing bad could ever happen to them because they were aware of their larger self, which never dies. When you are playing a video game character, you are actually safe at home even though you are fighting battles. This is how we felt.*

*But there are those of you who have a desire to be more immersed and strive for more detailed video games. Today you have massively multiplayer, role-playing games played in first person in a three-dimensional virtual environment. You interact with this environment and with other avatars in this "realm". It is far easier to forget you are actually at home, and someday, in the not too distant future, your video games that you know now will be much more immersive and you will have a more difficult time remembering that you are safe at home.*

*In a similar way, we felt that a more immersive experience would be better and that the evolution to be gained from the initial way of communicating with our fragment selves was not fast enough. So we tried several experiments and our most successful became the employment of the ego that we spoke of earlier. (Chapter 2: The Nature of the Soul) We developed the ego as a "foreman" in charge of the incarnation and also as a way of separating the experience of the soul-fragment from its spiritual source. We did this because if our fragment felt that it could be harmed, it would learn faster. If you touch a hot stove and it burns you but does not hurt much, you will not learn to not touch it. If there is more pain, you will learn faster. Is this clear?*

Yes, so the more intense the experience, the more experience there is to be gained.

*Yes, and also the more cut off from the entity one feels, the faster one can learn, in a sense. Now, of course we were a bit too successful with this ego. It is very practical in that it does create fast evolution. But we did not intend for the soul-fragment to NEVER remember that it is connected to us. It is difficult for the fragment when they can seldom take a break from this intense experience, and many of you leave sooner than you intended because you cannot stand the separation. In fact many of you would live longer lives if you could once in a while remember and feel the divine connection and the love surrounding you. Some of you feel alone and so you go home, you see. The soul-fragment is always a part of the larger soul entity and this separation creates the inherent desire for spiritual connection. This is the reason many feel so drawn to spiritual connection. It is also the reason that humans have created religion. Religion is a way of remembering and feeling the connection to your divine selves, your larger entity and loved ones, and [it's a way of] loving itself.*

*So, the ego in some cases is a bit too successful, but we are still working on this. There are those of you who recognize this and you attempt to make contact with your entity and to help remember, and you are helping us come up with ways to refine the ego. There are those of you who strive to put your ego aside, and who, through meditation, try to stretch your ego, try to ask it to step aside for a time so that you can convene with your true spirit. It is helpful for you to do this, and you can stay incarnated longer without feeling bereft or desolate or thinking that you are alone.*

*That is the short version.*

So, it seems a bit like a situation where our spiritual evolution has developed ways of increasing experience that intensify the immersion, but it has gone so far that it is sometimes actually detrimental to the evolution?

*Yes, in a sense. Because if a soul-fragment incarnation leaves early because it cannot stand the separation, then there goes the evolution. Not that you cannot evolve after death. You certainly can. However, your life is a very fast way to learn and if you cut it off, there goes your fast-track. An overbearing ego can create an intense desire for sensory experience and a separation of spiritual communication which can lead to addictions and unhappiness, respectively. Both of these can cut a life short.*

Right. That could explain a lot of accidents and suicides.

*Indeed.*

Now, has the ego evolved on its own or is it always engineered by entities?

*It has become its own sort of personality, if you will.*

Can we blame the ego for all of our problems?

*You can actually blame the ego for many of your problems. You can blame anything. However you would do well to remember that the ego is a big part of you. It is also part of me. It is us. But it is a part of us that we have separated by design and therefore it can become a bit of a monster.*

Right, because at least in my experience—and I hope that I can extrapolate this to others—this feeling of separation, this loneliness, this isolation creates discontent and frustration and can manifest itself in all kinds of negative behavior for us.

*Yes, it can deter your evolution if you are not feeling creative and snappy. If you are happy and creative, you can evolve very quickly this way. However, that is not to say that you cannot evolve from feeling desolate. There is something to be learned from every experience. You do not want to stay feeling desolate, however.*

You mentioned that the more primitive humans did not have the same type of ego. Is that why we think of a lot of primitive cultures as being superstitious and not so skeptical like more modern day thinkers?

*They were in some ways more sure of themselves because they understood they were not alone. They understood the connection of spirit; your modern thinkers can sometimes perceive this way of thinking as naive.*

But it's actually the other way around. Isn't it? Modern skeptics are naive in their disbelief of spiritual evolution.

*In a sense, this is true. Yes. But there are many things that could not have been developed as quickly without the ego.*

Right. Like awesome video games, for example?

*Yes.*

Now, another question. Say, as an example, along the lines of evolution: I live my life and have certain experiences and I finally cross over and I decide there's more experience I want to have, and say, for example, I spawn a new soul-fragment. Why would I not create a new soul that is more evolved, one with more evolved abilities than what I had before?

*You are free to do that if you wish.*

But it seems like that would be really advantageous.

*But you can only develop a more evolved self to the extent that you are evolved, you see. You cannot create something more evolved than yourself.*

But wouldn't I evolve throughout my lifetime, somehow on a personal level?

*Yes, of course. And the evolution will spread throughout your entity from you. But you are free to draw upon the evolution of your entity as well. But if you are personally creating the shard and not your entity, you will have to draw down from the entity through you, you see. So Shalkeera, in partnership with you, could likely create a more evolved shard than you personally alone could. Do you see?*

Right, okay. Because the larger entity has had more experience. That might answer my next question which is: even though it seems like we have more knowledge and there are many more smart people here, it seems like the majority of us are as dumb as ever.

*This is a question?*

Well, maybe it's a comment. The question is, why is this so? But I think you just answered it.

*It is because there are lesser shards doing the creating. We do not mean any disrespect when we use the term "lesser".*

Right. Well, I was going to say that I do not mean any disrespect when I use the word "dumb".

*Perhaps.*

So if Shalkeera and Brahma and only larger entities were doing all of the creating, everyone would be smart?

*Smarter.*

Smarter than some of the others who were created by soul-fragments.

*Yes, we have both evolved to the point where we can create "smarts", if you like. However there might be something to gain by creating a personality that is not so smart. Say you want to study emotional intelligence and felt that mind or mental intelligence might be a hindrance; you might create someone who is not so mentally sharp. You see.*

Right. OK.

*It depends upon the spiritual goal, of course. But sometimes you create these things unintentionally as well.*

## Human Evolution

Okay. I just scratch my head sometimes when I think of all of the humans out there today with barbaric behavior and violence and deception and I wonder why they aren't more evolved.

*There have been castoffs from lesser entities who wish to experience all this world has to offer. There are also larger entities who have sent those like you and many others who are more evolved into the world to help keep the world in balance, to temper these, as you say, "barbaric" actions.*

So part of the reason I'm here is to balance that out?

*Yes.*

Because from my small point of view it just seems like they're just ruining my world.

*But you are here to save it, you see. And there are others like you. There is an important contrast for you to experience. They will appreciate the world and your efforts in time.*

They're not making it easy.

*Indeed. It is part of your challenge and your evolution and your growth to find solutions to these problems.*

Okay. It just seems like there are more creative things that we would rather focus on than balancing out those who are destructive.

*You should focus on the problems you are drawn to focus on.*

Okay. That makes me feel better.

---

*We are looking towards a future where lesser entities or soul-fragments or shards if you are more connected to their greater entities. We are looking for a solution, a way to stretch the ego and to make it more flexible so that it will allow more communication between the entity and the soul-fragment experiencing this world. We believe now that evolution would be faster if there was more of a balance. We believe that those of you who are here to grow and experience and learn for us will stay longer if you have the love and support you need from us. We understand now that this love and support is very important to you. We did not realize how you would feel without it, or rather without the perception of it, because you do always have it. We did not anticipate it would be so important to remind you. And so, we are now looking to evolve spiritually into a future where you are more connected to your entities and your angels and your spirit guides so that it is a more easily flowing connection. This improved connection would not have so much trouble and not so many barriers blocking you from exploring your relationships with your helpers and your entity. We believe this will lead to greater, faster creativity. However, in your terms, it will seem like it is a long time in coming. There is much work to do on this. But this is what we are looking towards. Some of you are having some luck with this.*

Is any of this happening through religion or other spiritual activities?

*There is new age thinking that is helpful. We cannot say there is a concrete religion that is more helpful than general spirituality at this juncture. All the religions serve their purpose, and certainly some people are more hopeful with religion because of where their entity is, spiritually speaking.*

Would it be fair to say religious people are better off when they have their own personal relationship with their god, as they say, rather than just listening to what others are always preaching?

*Yes. This is much more advantageous. Those who look to a mediator such as a priest to speak to God for them do not have a direct connection and they [therefore] remove the power from themselves. But they do this because they are not yet ready to own up to the power that is theirs. It would be more helpful if they would do this. Specifically, to take responsibility and to understand that it is all* you. *Everything around you is a reflection of who you are in this moment and only you have the power to change it. It is malleable. It is not for some god to change unless* you *call upon this god to do so.*

It seems like somebody should write a manual on how to connect with your own god.

*Yes, perhaps that would be helpful.*

Even I need that.

*I see. Well you are free to ask me questions at this juncture.*

Right, but I feel like I am going through a mediator.

*Yes, indeed. In a sense you are.*

Rather than going through my own personal connection.

*Yes, indeed. Well, we encourage you to develop your own personal relationship. We have always encouraged this.*

So that's where we are headed?

*Yes, that is the goal, the general goal for all of us involved in this at this juncture.*

So you think if we have a better balance between our physical experience and our spiritual communication with our source energy, we will be much better off?

*Yes, we now believe this is a faster track to evolution.*

Now, sometimes you speak as though the future has already happened. Do you see it that way?

*In a sense, yes. It has already happened. The Brahma that is talking to you, however, is in a reality where it has not yet occurred. Do you understand?*

Sort of. Is that because it would be difficult for the Brahma of the future to speak to me?

*It could occur. Right now this part of me has connected with this part of Bronwen connecting to you right now. It is a good juncture. It is a good coordination of energies. To call a future energy into the mix would be possible but would be more challenging.*

Would it be difficult for me to understand the conversation?

*We can obtain some glimpses of this future which is why we can tell you this. However at this juncture, we are not technically from the future.*

Okay. So, for example, in the future, if we were more balanced with our source, would we be more apt to have visions or daydreams?

*Yes. This would occur with more frequency and they would be trusted, you see. And less people would be called crazy.*

Would some people have trouble differentiating a vision from a physical occurrence or knowing what is real and what is not?

*This is not the goal. The goal is to be able to differentiate, however. It is to understand the connection as real and know that is as real as this reality, though different. It is sort of like being on an airplane or being in your house. You know when you are on an airplane and you know when you are in your house and neither is less real to you.*

Right, we just know they're different.

*And yet when you are on an airplane you may not necessarily really understand what is going on unless perhaps you are the pilot.*

True.

*To some extent you know, but to another you do not know where you are in space and what coordinates of Earth you are above. You do not know necessarily the weather that you're going through or what is going on above or below you or even necessarily how the mechanics of it or the physics of it even work, even if you have some technical understanding. But you accept it as real even though all you see are the windows and the inside of the vehicle. You know it is different than your home, which you expect to remain stationary. So it is quite different.*

So, with respect to interpreting visions and understanding where we are, can we consider psychics to be much more evolved than skeptics?

*We would generally agree with that statement.*

And psychics are not crazy. Right?

*Some of them are, of course. However, there are many who are very much in touch with their intuition and therefore are very much evolved. They are here to help you.*

---

Now, it occurred to me that in looking toward a future where lesser entities or soul-fragments are more connected to greater entities, and in seeking solutions for faster evolution, one of the biggest problems of the ego seems to be the separation. It seems like channeling, what we are doing now, would be a great way for people to connect with their energies.

*It is indeed. It is very helpful and evolving. And were more people to do this type of exercise, it would be evolutionary for most of them.*

So can that be one solution for a faster evolution?

*Most certainly.*

But not everyone can do it though, right?

*Not everyone can accept this type of communication and many people would not believe themselves capable of it.*

Well, of course, but if many people who were already capable of it were doing it, that would increase the plausibility of it for the skeptics. It could make it more acceptable and believable.

*Yes, correct.*

So, maybe we should have classes and teach people how to connect to their spirit guides through methods like channeling.

*There are such classes available. They are just not available widely.*

But what if there was a school, for example, that could teach young people this?

*This could be very enlightening and very good.*

I'm thinking, a college class or some kind of new age school.

*Yes, it could solve many of your problems.*

Because it seems to me that the more people there are doing it, the more accepted it will be, and it could become a healthy practice for human consciousness on the whole.

*This is correct. As long as it is taught in the proper manner. And this means primarily accepting only the energies of wisdom and love in the communications.*

Is that because there could be a lot of chaotic energy that could be channeled?

*There could be false energies that could be found. Voices of fear or hatred are sometimes noticed by persons and these are not voices from your entity, not voices from a higher energy or spirit guide or an angel. So, distinguishing the voices would be important.*

Right.

*If they are negative, they have no validity and this must be understood. If they are disrespectful or harmful of any creature, then they are not authentic, and so authenticity should be strived for.*

Okay. So that helps me a lot in understanding the spiritual evolution. How does that translate into a physical evolution? Or is there any difference?

*Humans have, as a race, become heavier and denser. You will become lighter. You will become freer and, yes, you will become more physically able to run faster, to swim faster, to leap further and higher. Because you will be lighter, the energy will be less dense. It will change and therefore your physical body will change as well.*

Something like the elves of fantasy?

*In a sense, yes.*

Not the short, Santa Claus elves that make toys, but the tall, slender, lightweight, elves of Lord of the Rings.

*Yes. It will be more akin to this. Some of you are attracted to these elves for this reason. It is a glimpse of something that might be more like your future than you suspect. Though we do not believe the pointy ears will come into play. Probably.*

I'm sorry, but I just have a hard time visualizing the image of the future of America as being less dense and lighter weight.

*We are looking toward this goal. Let us just say that. We understand the human state is very dense at this point.*

I'm thinking of the increased prevalence of obesity.

*Indeed. Of course we are aware of this. There are those like you who are bucking to change the system and work for our good and our advantage. It is not advantageous for these people to eat what they eat and do what they do and live how they live. It is not making them happy. It is not making them evolve faster. But it is a valid experience that is worth experiencing.*

Maybe we are pushing a pendulum to get more momentum to swing in a better direction.

*That is the goal, yes. There are those of you who are our emissaries working toward this goal. Helping us to realize a better Earth, a better world, a better system of learning. A happier system as well. It is advantageous for you to make the most of your physical bodies while you are here. There is much that you will miss when you do not have them at your disposal. There is much physically that you miss now that you would be happy to regain. However, if you challenge yourself physically and make yours bodies strong, it will make you happier in general. It will give you a glimpse of the bodies of the future. They'll be stronger and lighter and more able to do things with less effort.*

Will this body of the future last longer?

*Yes, indeed. Which is advantageous to us and advantageous to the world. We do not want you to cross over and come home too quickly.*

Unless we're just messing things up?

*Of course, or unless that was the original plan. Which in some cases, of course, it is. Sometimes we will send a soul-fragment forth to make just one little tweak. And then we expect this fragment to come home. Just this one thing needs to be done. Just move this one rock. That is all that needs to be done and then you may come home. The fragment does not always return after this, but his work is done. It can decide to do something else if it chooses, or it can choose to come home. Sometimes this is the plan. Many times it is not.*

So that is a valid question that people ask when people are here for a short time. Maybe they were just here for a couple of reasons?

*Yes, for a seemingly small purpose or maybe a seemingly large one.*

Maybe we just can't see the whole influence of it?

*Indeed, yes. Sometimes moving a rock can change the whole course of world events.*

So, how much longer before I get superpowers?

*We imagine perhaps some future soul-fragment of yours will have such things. However, after you cross over, you are free to experience superpowers as you wish in the afterlife. You could be experiencing them now if you practice awakening in the dream state. Just decide what superpowers you want to have, take your consciousness with you, and you will remember when you return to your body. And you will feel as though you have had those superpowers. You will feel as though it happened to you yesterday. It will not feel like a dream. And it will give you confidence in your life. This is just a suggestion. You are not obligated to take our advice.*

I like the sound of that. If, like you say, our future holds more balance and a better connection to source, it occurred to me that trying to get the majority of human consciousness headed in that direction could be one reason for all of the violence and madness that I see in the world today. Perhaps there is a sort of exploration of that direction as an experience to allow human consciousness to see that that is not the direction to go. Does that sound like a correct assumption?

*That is one correct interpretation. This can yield the same result. Although it is possible to have a contagious directing of consciousness in a focused direction without pushing away from something.*

The only reason I can think of to explain the world's violence is the need to experience the contrast of what we do not want. There are always more cries for peace in the face of war.

*Yes it is always helpful to experience contrast. It creates growth, which is our goal.*

---

I can very much see in myself the idea you mentioned about really enjoying playing basic video games, but being frustrated that there aren't better graphics available and that there isn't a more immersive experience. I feel the same frustrations in life that I think many of us do; that we like this life but we want more. We want it to be better.

*We all do. We wish to be more physically able to rise to the challenges of this world and we wish to be, on the whole, happier and brimming with creativity.*

With more fulfillment?

*Yes. We will eventually see this happen and then we will see how well it works.*

*It is a continuing experiment, you see. A constant process of evolution. There have been other experiments, of course, and I feel I must mention the Lumanians. That was an experiment in another reality where we shunned all violence, and many of you who are seeking to be emissaries for us in this new goal are descended spiritually from those energies. This experiment, however, as idyllic as it sounds, did not offer the contrast necessary for evolution. We do not want so much of today's violence, but some of that seems to be a good catalyst for growth.*

A reminder of a balance and a direction to go?

*Yes. The world must be balanced. With no violence whatsoever the world lacked a certain vitality. It was a bit milquetoast you see, and not quite as exciting. And so the growth was not as rapid and the feelings were not as intense and intensity facilitates evolution.*

Is that like how overcoming an easy challenge does not provide as much satisfaction as a difficult challenge?

*Yes, indeed. There have been various experiments that we have participated in. The experiment with the Lumanians was one of them. You might think of Atlantis as being a past world. It is actually more of a sister world. It exists and that experiment sometimes seems to be going rather well. It is difficult to explain because I see the past and the future and the present of this world at the same time. They were very advanced in technology and moved larger objects with sound, and light was used for healing and energy balancing. But they went a bit too far with the technology and caused their own destruction in this way. However it is difficult to say this since it still participates in its own time and continues to build upon itself. One reality of Atlantis destroys itself, you see.*

And they were not here on Earth?

*No, they existed on an Earth similar this one. It is similar to a probable world where some significant events happened and yet nearly happened in a probability. In this hypothetical situation, both future paths were equally probable, and therefore the momentum of the energies carried on a probability down both paths, splitting into two realities. This can create duplicate worlds which can continue to evolve in different ways creating similar but different worlds in separate alternate universes.*

I am still wrestling with the probability idea, but I am beginning to grasp the concept. And the Atlanteans weren't underwater people?

*No, Atlantis was a large island, is a large island.*

We have many versions of Atlantis mythologies.

*The people of Atlantis were highly developed and very intelligent. Sometimes there are avenues available at "coordination points" on your world where you can see glimpses of this. Sometimes they give you, on this plane, in this world, ideas for technological advances. This is why you have mythologies. There have been spiritual or mental communications between your worlds and there have also been physical interactions through coordination points many years ago in your history. Again, we will speak at length about coordination points and mythologies in another book.*

And you mentioned the Lumanians; did they exist here on Earth?

*In a sense, they did.*

So in a sense they are part of our history?

*Yes, in a sense. It is not exactly the same Earth but one that is similar enough.*

But it had an influence?

*Yes, because it was of our energy. Many energies that now create your Earth, that now participate in it, also participated in the Lumanian experience or experiment, if you will. You see, we are always trying things. We are always dabbling in reality, asking, "What will make the best experience? What will evolve us faster?"*

Much like a video game programmer who both programs and plays the game?

*Indeed. Though Lumania is very dear to us.*

And some of us are more closely descended spiritually from Lumania?

*Yes, indeed.*

Do I know anyone who is a spiritual descendant?

*There are many, many of you who have some spiritual traits of the Lumanians. You know Bronwen, of course. You also have some of this energy in you. Bronwen has more of it. You have seen how she has an adverse reaction to violence. In this respect, she has much of this energy in her personality. You may notice it in others as you look at champions of non-violence and peace, like Gandhi and Mother Teresa.*

I think that gives us not only a bit of where we are headed evolutionarily, but a little on how we have gotten here. Thank you for your insight.

*You are more than welcome.*

# CHAPTER 12
## OUR RELATIONSHIPS WITH ANIMALS

Brahma has said that relationships are the most important thing we have on this planet and most of us have very important relationships with other humans. However, relationships with animals are also very important to some people, and in this discussion Brahma tells us about how these relationships can benefit humans spiritually. In this chapter we get a glimpse of their importance from Brahma's point of view as well as learning about the spiritual significance of certain animals.

So, how important are human relationships with nonhuman animals?

*In many cases they are far more important than most humans realize and it is a topic that is of clear importance to both you and Bronwen.*

Yes. You could call us animal lovers.

*Indeed, if we were to define true animal lovers on this planet, we would have to include you two in that group.*

In general, how do relationships with animals differ from the relationships with humans?

*Animals are a different type of energy from you. They are almost like a different species of energy. It is similar to the difference between the angels and humans. All beings are of course composed of energy. However, those who incarnate as animals are a different type of energy who have chosen to incarnate with you on this planet for the purpose of evolving and learning. There are also the dolphins and whales which are additionally a different variety of energy from you or from most other animals.*

So dolphins and whales are different from dogs, spiritually speaking?

*Yes. The dolphins and whales, the cetaceans, are as different from animals as you are from them. Though make no mistake, all the energies do have similarities. We realize that you are all animals biologically, but since most of our perspective involves the spiritual aspects of animals, we will use the term "animal" to refer to non-human and non-cetacean animals.*

Okay. Now, we usually consider animals as having stronger instincts than humans. Does that mean they are more in touch with their larger selves?

*Generally, the energies of animals are much more in touch with their source energy than you are. You and other humans have largely chosen linear thinking as your way to navigate this world. Now, we are not including cetaceans, the whales and dolphins, when we are speaking about animals here. Animals generally choose a more immediate and emotional way of thinking than your linear way, which separates you more from your source than does the way of the animals. You are not superior to them as some might imagine. You are just different.*

So, does that mean they have less influential egos?

*Yes. This is correct. They have a different type of ego. It is not nearly as developed as your own.*

They seem to be less separated consciously from things. They seem to know how to do a lot of stuff without being taught. Birds and fish know where to migrate without their parents and cats don't need to be potty trained like dogs and humans.

*They have a different type of learning than you do. Of course both spiritual species are born with innate knowledge. But animals tend to retain that type of thinking, while humans tend to develop linear types of thinking which enable their egos to disconnect more, which then allows them to grow and have more power. It is just a different way of thinking and learning.*

Okay. So, how is the experience of animals different from the experience of a human?

*They are more Zen, if you will permit the analogy, because they live in the moment. They do not think very much about the past and the future. They are able to live for now. Living in the present is something many humans strive to accomplish. Many humans spend their entire lifetimes trying for this goal, whereas in most animals it is innate. They live in the moment and accept experiences as they are without projecting possible consequences of the past or concerns of the future on the present moment, mostly just enjoying it for the present experience. This is not to say of course, that animals cannot be affected by past memories or worries of the future. They can, and some animals can get traumatized as well. However, for the most part, even when a trauma has occurred, they live in the moment. They are not completely crushed by unfulfilled expectations and they can forgive easier that humans can.*

*Also, animals have an innate sense when they are born that they deserve love and that they are loved by their entity. They feel worthy automatically. In contrast, many humans feel as though they must earn love and worthiness.*

Is that because humans are more separated from their spiritual cheerleading section and their larger entity?

*Yes, that is the reason. But this separation can be offset by humans' relationships with animals. Connections with animals can remind humans of their own worthiness and that they are loved unconditionally. Humans forget this when they feel disconnected from divine source and the spiritual love that is always there. Animals and humans have much to offer each other. It can be a relationship of mutual benefit.*

So that explains why therapy animals can have such great results.

*Yes, and they are helping reform your society's outcasts, those locked up in prisons, in places where there are prison animal programs.*

Okay.

Now, do animal souls have a larger entity similar to the way humans souls do?

*Yes.*

So each new animal soul-fragment comes from a larger, animal-entity soul?

*It comes from a type of entity. Yes, it works the same way, but as I said it is a different type of energy. It is similar to yours, but animal entities do not generally incarnate as humans. They may get there if they choose, though this is not often the case. It is more often that a human entity would choose to have an animal incarnation.*

Does that have anything to do with humans being more evolved spiritually? Wait, maybe I should ask, are humans more evolved?

*They are differently evolved. We cannot say that either type of energy is more evolved than the other. The animals are more evolved in certain ways.*

Of course.

*And humans are more evolved in others. The animals, for instance, are more evolved in these ways: They do not judge and they accept love if love is offered, and they love freely. Humans are much more cautious to love, and offer judgment quite frequently.*

Yes, human love often comes with a lot of conditions.

*Yes. And there is criticism and judgment, whereas in the animal world this does not happen with such frequency. Naturally, it does occur, but not in the same way. Animals will not usually judge based solely on looks or on species. They will judge based on their experience with another, for the most part. They do not judge humans who harm them very often. If there is love, frequently, they still will love them even if they are harmed. It is a non-conditional love. You humans seldom have this.*

No, we hold grudges.

*Yes, and put strict conditions on your love.*

And we often withhold our love.

*Yes, animals see no reason to do this.*

So you mentioned that we have much to gain from animals and they can benefit from us as well.

*Yes.*

Do you mean that we can benefit from our experience with them here on Earth?

*That is correct. They can teach humans how to be present in a moment, how to accept other energies for what they are, and help to love without condition. If you pay attention to the animals, they teach you this. You love your cat, unconditionally. Sometimes he does things that upset you, but you cannot bring yourself to not love him because of these things even when he is doing some things that really irk you. You know how to love him and to treat him with kindness. Because of your relationship with him, he is showing you this way of acceptance, this way of living. You cannot always extend this to other humans, but at least you can do this with certain animals that you interact with.*

I know, but that is because he is so much cuter than most humans and I can't stay mad at him.

*Indeed. This is one of their tools with which they teach.*

Sometimes when I look at other people it is easy to find things to hate about them, but when I look at cats I just cannot hate no matter what they do.

*Cuteness is a tool. It allows them to teach you and allows you to teach them. Also, when you do get mad at them and perhaps yell at them, they may react, but soon they will be looking at you with love. You may still be upset with them, but since they will have moved past the disagreement and are back to loving, you will have trouble staying mad at them. Humans on the other hand, tend to throw anger back and forth between each other and perpetuate the disagreement.*

I see that animals can do much for us. What do humans do that is good or is beneficial for animals?

*Animals can benefit in relationships with humans who are in good relationships with them. They can learn different ways of thinking about things. You can teach them how to think a little bit more linearly which they may not otherwise come to do. You can teach them how to be in a relationship with a human that is unlike any relationship they will find with another animal on this planet. Humans are quite different creatures in the ways of their relationships. Animals like to watch humans in the same way that humans like to watch animals. Animals are very curious about human behavior and they are very curious about what humans will do next. They find life with humans very exciting and unpredictable. They are very happy when humans show them affection and play with them because they find it very stimulating.*

Or maybe hilarious. I imagine that watching humans from the point of view of those little animals could be very entertaining.

*They are indeed very entertained by you and because you are often large in comparison with them, they literally look up to you.*

So, to them, not only are we entertaining fools, but we are big fools. When I think about it, it seems like watching humans from any non-human perspective could be hilarious.

*Animals are very curious to see what their humans will do next when they have a close relationship with a human, and they thrill with the attention the human gives them. They learn different ways of thinking, different ways of being, and different ways of interacting. You realize that the relationship that you have with your cats is not the kind of relationship that a cat could ever have with another cat. It is a completely different sort of relationship. Cats don't meow to each other the way they meow to humans. Your cat's relationship with you is similar to a kitten's relationship to his mother, or a puppy's relationship to her mother, but it goes way beyond this and they do not outgrow this relationship as they age. Although, often dogs are more intense companions than cats are; this can vary and cats can be closer to humans than dogs. It all depends on the relationship, the circumstance, and the individuals involved.*

So, from a spiritual point of view, should everyone have pets?

*It is beneficial if humans can find an animal that they like to connect with on a regular basis. If humans find they do not like any animals, then it is best perhaps to not have any for the time being.*

Okay another question. I know it's a long shot but I have to ask: How do I translate cat language?

## Our relationships with Animals

*The animals think in pictures. So you must look into their eyes and see what picture they are giving you. You must hear with your spiritual senses as well. Look into their eyes and hear with your spirit and find the picture they are giving you.*

Okay, I will try that.

Why are there so many human relationships with cats and dogs and very few relationships, statistically, with all the other animals?

*There are many wild animals that cannot be tamed. Naturally, there are many animals other than cats and dogs that can be tamed. Of these animals, dogs and cats and horses are of most use to humans and so humans have cultivated these relationships. Humans could cultivate relationships with many types of the animals that are tamable. I will add that although there are a few wild animals that are not considered to be tamable, a select few of that group would be tamable in the right circumstances with the right humans. But that does not mean you should go try to tame every snake that you see. Most of them are very wild. But the animals that are of most use to humans have become the most popular to have relationships with. Historically, dogs were good for hunting and retrieving and protecting a flock and standing guard. Cats were useful for ridding food supplies of pests. Horses, of course, were good for transportation but they are not as easy to live with as dogs or cats.*

*This all is from the point of view of humans who can choose to have relationships with animals or not. Animals generally are open to relationships with humans but it is the humans who most often have the power to decide because of their position in this society. You could have a close relationship with a rat or a pig, for example, but most humans do not because they do not see pigs as having any real use to them in a companionship sort of way.*

Most people?

*Most. But there are a few pet owners of pigs who enjoy their company immensely.*

Of course. Yes, the only use that I can think of for pigs is to use them for finding truffles.

*Yes, there are a few that are used for this purpose. They are not generally pets, however.*

Right. So it seems as though the primary reason that we have had relationships with animals is because of their practical usefulness, like you mentioned. I'm

~ 215 ~

also thinking of cows and oxen used to pull plows for agriculture or donkeys for carrying.

*Yes, although they are largely no longer needed for this purpose.*

Now, the biggest question that I have is: How is it that animals like cows, who were once useful for pulling plows, never became companion animals and now are only used for meat, milk, and leather, while cats and dogs can now be of almost no practical use yet they are treasured as family members?

*It is cultural. There are societies, as you may remember, that do eat cats and dogs. It is America and some other societies that do not. Americans have grown very attached to their dogs and their cats and they see them as being on par with their other family members. So, of course in this case, eating them would be unthinkable. But in certain societies on your planet today they are raised for food.*

And of course there are societies that do not eat cows.

*Yes, in India primarily.*

But how did we get into the habit of eating our tamed animals? Do we eat other animals simply because humans witnessed some predator animals eat them and we saw it as a natural behavior, or is there a better reason for why humans eat animals? I ask because personally, I see no reason to kill and eat animals, but I know that everyone has different reasons for doing things.

*Humans eat animals because they do not know any better. They have seen animals eat other animals and some humans believe this is the way, the correct way, the best way to live life.*

Is this true? Is it the best way to live?

*Humans are not biologically designed to eat animals very often and certainly not as often as you eat them today as a collective society. Humans were meant to BE ABLE to digest animals in the event that there was no fresh food available to be able to survive if there was nothing growing from the ground. And this would only be a holdover until something started to grow from the ground and was edible for humans. But in an earlier time, when things would no longer grow from the ground, man would go to the sea to find sea kelp and seaweed and such like that to eat, and occasionally a fish was caught and eaten also and was found to be a good source of protein when there were no edible plants for man to eat. This is how it was meant to be: as a survival mechanism when times were harsh; it was not to be consumed as an everyday event.*

*There is no excuse for what is going on today. The mass genocide of these creatures is blasphemy. It is not meant to be this way and it is certainly much different from a man who is living in the forest and starving and kills one animal to consume to survive through the winter. It is quite different. Humans were not meant to live in frozen places where plants cannot grow. They are not biologically suited to cold climates. Human skin is equipped with sweat glands for cooling but does not have much fur that is resistant to the cold.*

So it is barbaric for humans to eat animals?

*We are not saying that it is barbaric for humans to eat animals; we are saying that what is happening with your factory farms now is barbaric. We are saying that humans can eat animals if circumstances dictate and only in times of dire need.*

So, what is the reason then that humans do this? And I guess a similar question is: Why do humans exploit animals the way that they do?

*Humans do this because they can. They feel more powerful if they have control over other creatures. It is similar to how the school bully feels. He needs to prop himself up with those he feels are weaker than him so that he can feel stronger. It is actually indicative of weakness because the school bully is too weak to get power from himself. He needs to take it from others.*

So it is some form of insecurity?

*Yes. "I need to prove that I am stronger than this mouse so I will kill the mouse." This is not, of course, the case with a cat. The cat will eat the mouse because the cat is hungry. And this is what cats were meant to eat. Humans kill to feel superior and killing larger animals placates larger insecurities. But humans were not meant to eat or kill other animals except in dire circumstances. Humans were meant to eat plants that grow from the ground and those that grow in the sea as well.*

So this is like a bully dominating a smaller schoolmate or more powerful groups of people exploiting other disadvantaged groups of people to feel superior. Exploiting or killing animals is basically the same thing, correct?

*Yes, it is a very similar thing.*

For the same insecure reasons?

*Yes, this is correct. Humans have not yet learned that when they harm the animals, they harm themselves. The different acts of inflicting harm are of similar energy. Every action that you take, and every corresponding reaction that the animals have, reverberates throughout the universe and affects all energies, not just energies of the human ilk. Energies of the animal ilk affect yours as well and vice versa. The energy, though different on the surface, at its very core is all one. Different species and breeds of energy, if you go back far enough, will converge into one energy. It is a unified field of influence, you see. And if you harm one thing, you harm us all.*

*Now, if we come back to the situation where there is a man living by himself in the woods and there is no food left growing in the ground, if the man has been respectful of Earth and does not generally take more than he needs, sometimes an agreement will be made. If he feeds himself the plants that he needs and does not rape Earth of all of the plants, but leaves what he can to grow again, and there is no more food despite this, sometimes an animal will agree to let go of its life to feed this man. This could happen especially if this man is beneficial in some way to the forest. These types of agreements can be made, you see.*

Is that what happens in the wild with predators and prey?

*Very often it is an agreement. Yes. Sometimes there are accidents, or prey is taken by surprise and it will always seem this way. However, very often in the wild it has been agreed upon at a spiritual level. The weakest wildebeest is sick and it knows it is slowing down the herd. A lion appears nearby. Not only is it easier for it to catch the weakest wildebeest, but the weakest wildebeest will sometimes be willing to let its life go in order to save the herd. It does not want to feel the burden of responsibility for slowing the entire herd down or causing the deaths of healthy members of the herd that have more life to live when the wildebeest, who is ill, knows that it has not much time left in any case.*

Right. Okay. That's a huge contrast from what humans are doing today.

*Yes, indeed it is.*

Why is it then that so few people are vegetarians?

*They do not understand the consequences of their actions. They do not understand what it does to themselves and we do not mean just physically. Although there are physical consequences, it also harms them spiritually.*

So nutritional effects aside, what if somebody experiences such spiritual harm, do they get some sort of spiritual injuries? And can that result in physical harm also?

*Yes, and it can result in physical illnesses and deformities, diseases of the body. Now, again, we are not speaking of the man in the forest, that is a different scenario and he will not experience spiritual harm if he kills an animal to eat when there is nothing else. Unless of course, he believes he will be harmed by the action, and in this case he should not. Belief can also have an effect.*

So humans should only harm animals when it is required for their survival and only with the spiritual agreement of the animal that presents itself?

*Yes, the ancient Native Americans were much more in tune with this philosophy. They would occasionally kill bison or deer and other animals like this, but usually it was to stow away for the winter when there was a need. They would use every single part of the animal and they would apologize to the animal and bless its spirit before it left the earthly plane. They would wish it well on its journey and thank it for its sacrifice. They did not eat nearly as much meat as most would imagine. They were mostly plant eaters who also ate meat when they felt that plants would be scarce, for the most part.*

Like in the winter?

*Yes.*

Okay. That makes sense.

---

So, you mentioned whales and dolphins. What can you tell me about their significance?

*They are spiritual types of animals that are closer to you than the other animal types, dogs and cats and the like. They are extremely intelligent and they are much closer spiritually to humans. So close, in fact, that killing a whale or a dolphin is on par with the offense of killing another human. They are very similar to you except they live in the oceans and cannot build things in the way that humans do.*

*However, they do build things with their minds and they also communicate in ways that you cannot even imagine with other cetaceans and other creatures in the ocean. They have a great effect on the climate and the general energy and the aura of Earth. They keep a balance with the planet that allows the seas to stay calm and the weather mild. They have effects on this planet that you humans do not even realize. To eradicate them would be a great crime not just for them and all animals but for all humanity as well.*

How do they build things with their minds?

*They create an atmosphere that is suitable for you to breathe and suitable for them as well, as they breathe air like you do. They create this with their minds. You help create it as well but they concentrate on it more. They are very instrumental in creating your atmosphere and your temperature and your earthly conditions. Things that make the planet habitable are in some part attributed to these creatures. They build a habitable environment.*

So you're saying they create from a mental or spiritual aspect?

*Yes. This is what I'm saying.*

Obviously they don't have fin-hands and little hammers and nails making oxygen machines.

*They do not build structures. They build with their spiritual minds. Humans create by manipulating physical matter as well as creating circumstance or happiness. They create in a more subtle way. They are creators of the environment.*

They create with more of a reality manifestation?

*Yes, of the atmosphere and environment.*

---

So, sometimes humans capture dolphins and put them in tanks and put them on display. From what you have told me, that sounds like it would be one of the worst things someone could do.

*One should not capture them from the wild. This is not acceptable.*

Does that mean that if someone were to breed them in captivity, the ones that would be born there would have somehow agreed to make that possible?

*Yes, this is correct. They would understand the circumstances into which they would be born and they would accept it.*

Otherwise it just wouldn't work?

*Yes, dolphins would not be able to breed in captivity if this were the case. There would be no willing souls and all of the breeding attempts would fail. Yet remember that not all creatures want to live out in the open sea, just as not all humans want to live free. Sometimes the energy just wants a small taste of things and is too scared to venture very far. In this case they might pick a situation similar to a dolphin community created in some sort of dolphin park.*

So, in captivity, they could possibly benefit from a relationship with humans?

*Absolutely they can, but some of the hardcore animal rights people, though they are well meaning, do not understand the benefits that some of these animals get from their relationships with humans. There are dolphins that will incarnate into a captive breeding zone just for a relationship they can have with a particular human that they could not otherwise have had in the wild, just as there are pets that will incarnate into your reality just to be a companion to a particular human for a part of a lifetime.*

Okay. So, can we communicate with dolphins the same way we might speak with cats and dogs? Do they think in pictures as well or are they totally different?

*They think in pictures and also in a type of energy that is very difficult to explain. It is more of a thought-energy. It is not a spoken word. It is similar to the way the angels communicate—with inclinations and thoughts—but they are not linear. They do not require any language. This is how they think. Now, of course they have a language of their own that includes sounds, which some of your humans are trying to translate. The sounds are manifestations of their energy thoughts. And the reason they make sound at all is because it is sometimes necessary for the sound to travel great distances to reach another dolphin.*

So it could be a much more effective means of communicating than what we have?

*It is a different way of communicating. But, yes, they can send their thoughts directly to another dolphin. If it is not paying attention because it is involved in other activities, it may not hear. However, it will hear a sound coming from far away from another dolphin.*

Right, Okay.

*If it hears the sound it can then communicate in thought. It is sometimes just a way to get attention. And they all have names of course, which are sounds by which they can identify each other. Each is unique.*

Okay. What about species that are not whales and dolphins? I'm thinking of other aquatic mammals like sea lions and seals and the walrus. Are those similar at all or are they totally different?

*They are on par with the other animals, most of the animals.*

They are not like the cetaceans?

*That is correct.*

Okay. So, should I avoid going to the theme park, Sea World?

*You must do what your conscious dictates. There are very good things that this company does and things that we do not agree with as well.*

Much like the behavior of all of humanity?

*This is correct. It is not a black and white situation.*

---

Now, I have often heard it said that the animals should be given special consideration because they aren't like humans, because humans can be considered to be masters of their own destiny, whereas animals are often subject to human control. Are any animals actually masters of their own destiny?

*In some ways they are not and in some ways they are, but they do not realize that they are. It depends on the individual animal. Many times when animals come into contact with humans who are kind to them, who are beneficial to them, they will begin to realize that they are in control of their own destiny. There are, of course, some animals born that already know this, but not all of them.*

So would dolphins and whales have a similar spiritual intelligence level as, say, chimpanzees and gorillas?

*They are similar in intelligence to humans.*

Chimpanzees and gorillas are similar to humans?

*Cetaceans are similar to humans.*

So whales and dolphins are more intelligent than gorillas and chimpanzees?

*Yes, according to your human standards of intelligence, spiritual intelligence.*

Right, but I mean spiritually.

*Well, let us be clear that no species is superior to another. Even your dogs and cats are not inferior to you. They are just different and they have different skills and masteries than you do. You just have more command of your environment. They are not inferior spiritually.*

Are cetaceans as evolved with regard to the ego as humans are?

*They are evolved in different ways. We cannot put one above the other, though I know you humans very much like to do this.*

I guess I do, too. We do have a tendency to try to rank or classify things in order to understand them.

*Yes, but it is as though you are comparing apples and oranges. It is a different thing. The apple has different strengths than the orange. And the orange, no matter how hard it tries, will never be an apple. The apple will never be an orange.*

But apples are better than oranges, in my opinion.

*This is, of course, a personal taste and everyone is entitled to their opinion. But it does not mean that one is better than the other as a universal truth. It may be perceived as better for you specifically, Robert.*

Right, we do need to consider the other opinions out there.

*Opinions are just opinions. They do not matter to the truth.*

They aren't just interpretations of the truth? Are you saying that the truth is separate?

*They are interpretations to you; however, the truth—the validity and the integrity—of one species of animals is not threatened by someone thinking less of it. Though many humans regard pigs as the lowest of the low, this does not in any way change the spiritual worthiness of pigs.*

---

Okay. Is there anything that you would like to say about our relationship with the animals that people need to hear?

*It is always beneficial to treat every creature, including other humans, every animal, every insect, even every blade of grass, with the same consideration that you would treat your best friend. One should always be respectful of every single form of life. It does not matter if you intend to eat this creature that is in front of you. You must still show it respect and love if you can. Again, we do not recommend the killing and eating of animals unless the circumstances demand it. It is harmful to treat any creature with disdain or disrespect because, if you do this, you are disdaining and disrespecting yourself. It is a reflection of how you feel about yourself when you do things to other creatures. And so if you treat other creatures with respect and love it is evidence that you respect and love yourself. This love and respect is beneficial to you and all of those in your immediate environment. Respect is our foremost recommendation to all.*

That is very well put. Thank you.

*Thank you.*

# ABOUT THE AUTHORS

## Robert H. Skye

Ever since he received his degree in philosophy, Robert H. Skye has been interested in all kinds of philosophy and spirituality.

He spends his free time birding and loves being in nature. He also likes superheroes and fantasy because he knows there's more to all of us than meets the eye.

Robert is a huge animal lover and tea aficionado who loves traveling, cooking, and technology. He spends a lot of time traveling and enjoys meeting people from all walks of life. He currently lives in Florida with his wife and rescued cats.

## Bronwen Skye

Bronwen Skye has starred in commercials, music videos, and made-for-TV movies. She earned her fine arts degree in Theater from Marymount Manhattan College in New York City. She is the author and contributing author of several books, including fiction, nonfiction, and satiric poetry.

True to having broadened her horizons at an early age by spending some of her developmental childhood years in Africa, she is a professional traveler, and vegan food connoisseur. Following a move to Southern California, she wrote and hosted a New Age radio show called Insight on AM 1460, and wrote an Op-Ed piece on the meaning of New Age thought for the Santa Monica Outlook.

When she's not traveling around the country, she spends her time reading and writing fantasy young adult fiction. A fanatic for all things Disney, she now lives in the Sunshine State.

Thank you for reading. I hope you enjoyed this material.

If you found any of it helpful, please consider helping us out. I need your feedback to help make our next book better. I'm only human right now. Please leave an honest review on Amazon.com. Tell us what you liked and how we can improve.

If you want to stay in touch and give us some private comments you can get in touch with us at www.skyedialogues.com.

If you are searching for more content, go to www.skyedialogues.com to see our latest publications, including our next book

*Karmic Law of Attraction: A Channeled Explanation of Auras and Positive Living*

Again, thank you so much for reading.

Printed in Great Britain
by Amazon